APPROVED!

Study Guide & Workbook

Alan R. Stewart (Author)

Adam R. Stewart (Author/Editor)

FUNDING SUCCESS

TEACHING ENTREPRENEURS HOW TO FUND THEIR BUSINESS

Approved! Study Guide & Workbook

Published by Funding Success, a division of FIT Advisors, LLC

ISBN: 978-0-9863553-3-2

Typography, Front and Back Cover Design by Adam R. Stewart

Infographics created in conjunction with Catherine Pham and the creative team at Infographic B2B.

Illustrations created by Liston Morris @Listoonzsurftoonz

TABLE OF CONTENTS

TABLE OF CONTENTS

$\mathcal{W}$elcome to the official Approved! Study Guide & Workbook!

With this workbook, you will put to practice the concepts, principles, skills, and strategies introduced in ***Approved! The Insider's Guide to Getting Your Bank Loan Approved***. The exercises and response questions were chosen and tailored to emphasize the key concepts that all entrepreneurs should understand as they undergo the business bank loan application process. In fact, students and self-taught entrepreneurs alike will find that many of the short responses and projects can be modified for future use in real-life business scenarios.

As you begin this journey, you will be introduced to a variety of new concepts, terms, and strategies – many of which might be unfamiliar to you. You should actively utilize this study guide as you read through **Approved!** Be sure to take notes in the provided note sections of this study guide (located at the end of each chapter) and don't forget to write down any questions or comments you have.

Each chapter in the study guide includes several exercise sections intended to help you become more familiar with the core concepts and terminology used throughout **Approved!** Specifically, the exercises are intended to test both your quantitative knowledge (definitions, facts, etc.) as well as your understanding of qualitative principles (leadership skills, critical reasoning, rationale, implications, etc.)

Each chapter also includes one or more Case Studies and Discussion Topics that can be used to improve your understanding of the real-life requirements and expectations that come with starting and running a business. These discussion topics will stimulate critical thought and reflect challenges that you may face in real-world business situations.

Lastly, many of the questions in the workbook relate specifically to "your business" and the funding requirements, banking needs, challenges and concerns of your business. For readers without an actual business, you should "create" a hypothetical business and answer the questions for that business.

We hope that you find **Approved! Study Guide & Workbook** to be a valuable supplement to **Approved!** If you have any comments, questions, or suggestions for future topics, please do not hesitate to let us know.

UNIT #1

CH. 1 – CH. 4

Ch. 1: Do I Need A New Bank?
Identifying the Bank Categories | Small vs Large Banks | Assessing Your Needs

Ch. 2: Meet the Banking Team
Your First Meeting | Key Personnel | The Banking Relationship

Ch. 3: Bank Loans – Advantages and Disadvantages
Understanding How Loans Work | Benefits & Downsides | Alternatives to Bank Debt

Ch. 4: Small Business Administration (SBA) Loan Programs
SBA Loan Options | Advantages, Requirements, & Disadvantages | Specialized SBA Loan Programs

CHAPTER 1: DO I NEED A NEW BANK?

INTRODUCTION

Congratulations! You are on your way to successfully understanding the bank loan application process. In Chapter 1, you became familiar with the different categories of banks and their associated characteristics, benefits, and downsides. As you prepare to complete the following exercises, think about what you learned about each category of bank. Consider how well each type of bank could satisfy your specific banking needs, such as funding requirements, desired ancillary services, or flexibility (among other things). You should also begin thinking about specific questions you would want to ask during your first meeting with a bank.

LEARNING OBJECTIVES

After reading chapter 1 and completing the review exercises in this unit of the study guide, you will be able to:

- Identify and describe each category of bank and the key characteristics for each category

- Compare and contrast the different bank categories as well as how large banks and small banks differ in terms of how they lend and what services they offer

- Define and describe ancillary bank services and identify potentially useful ancillary services

- Consider how well each type of bank can satisfy one's specific banking needs, such as funding requirements, desired ancillary services, and overall flexibility

- Prepare a list of potential questions to ask a prospective bank in order to get a better idea of how that bank operates and serves small businesses/entrepreneurs

HOW DO I SELECT A BANK?

CATEGORIES OF BANKS

- Community banks
- Regional or multi-regional banks
- Multinational banks
- Credit unions

BANKS ARE CATEGORIZED BY ASSETS UNDER MANAGEMENT & NUMBER OF RETAIL

HOW DO I FIGURE OUT WHICH BANK IS BEST FOR MY BUSINESS?

Start with your current bank & ask yourself the following questions:

- Are you happy with the service they provide?
- Do you have a positive relationship with the banking team?
- Can they provide your business the services you need as you grow?

Ancillary Bank Services You May Need As Your Business Grows

- Cash Management (Checking, savings, payroll)
- Retirement planning services (401K, deferred compensation plans, etc.)
- International banking assistance (Letters of credit)
- Subordinated debt (Mezzanine funding)
- Private equity placement
- Financial advisory services
- Mortgage loans and servicing
- Credit cards
- Wealth management and private client services
- Insurance services
- Capital lease and equipment financing

Larger Banks

- Provide more ancillary services
- Have robust software platforms
- Generally have better security
- Provide more online services
- Have more retail branch locations

Smaller Banks & Credit Unions

- Tend to be more "family-like"
- Can be more accommodating and flexible
- May provide more competitive rates on loans and deposits
- Have less branch office locations
- Offer fewer ancillary services
- Are non-profit organizations [Credit Unions Only]
- Only accept members if they meet certain eligibility requirements [Credit Unions Only]

A. VOCABULARY MATCH

Match the term to the correct definition

		Answer
1.	Local / Community Banks	1. ____
2.	Regional / Multi-Regional Banks	2. ____
3.	Multinational Banks	3. ____
4.	Credit Unions	4. ____
5.	Ancillary Services	5. ____

A. The largest category of bank, these banks tend to offer the most ancillary services and branch locations.

B. Unlike traditional banks, these are actually member-owned non-profit organizations and subject to membership requirements.

C. The smallest category of bank in terms of assets under management and number of branch locations.

D. Additional services offered by the bank and usually related to financial assistance, wealth management, or other services intended to assist your business.

E. Along with local community banks, this category of bank tends to be more accommodating and flexible compared to a large multinational bank.

B. TRUE OR FALSE

1. ___ The four primary categories of banks are community banks, regional banks, multinational banks, and international banks

2. ___ Regional banks are the smallest type of bank in terms of assets under management and number of retail branches

3. ___ Small banks and large banks usually offer the same amount of ancillary bank services

4. ___ Large multinational banks approve close to 50% of loan requests while small community banks approve only about 20%

5. ___ Credit unions are actually non-profit organizations rather than true banks

6. ___ Credit unions have historically focused more on consumer loans and less on business lending

C. Fill in the Blank

1. The smallest categories of banks in terms of both assets under management and number of retail branches are _____, followed by _____.

2. In addition to commercial loans, most banks offer many _____ such as cash management and retirement planning services.

3. Smaller community banks and regional banks will tend to be more _____ and _____ so the additional services offered by larger banks may be less important.

4. In general, community banks and small regional banks approve close to _____% of their loan requests while large multinational banks approve only about _____%.

5. Credit Unions tend to be more accommodating and family-like since they are _____.

6. Credit Unions have historically focused more on _____, meaning they participated less in small business lending.

KEY THEMES & CONCEPTS:

- Think about the various characteristics, positives, and negatives associated with each of the primary types of banks
- Examine the basic profile and qualities / characteristics of a typical small business owner / entrepreneur seeking bank financing for the first time
- Consider the reasons an entrepreneur may want to seek financing from one type of bank over another
- Think about which bank is the best fit for this particular individual – why is it a good fit, what does it offer that gives it an advantage over other banks, why is this preferable for less-established entrepreneurs, etc.

SHORT ANSWER

1. In your own words, briefly describe the different categories of banks. Compare and contrast the strengths and weaknesses for each category. Which type of bank might be the best fit for your own business?

_____
_____
_____
_____

2. In addition to traditional checking & savings accounts, most banks offer ancillary services such as financial planning and wealth management services. Read the list of ancillary services on pg. 23 and identify at least two services that you might use in the future. Why might these be important as your business grows?

_____
_____
_____
_____

3. Now that you understand the unique characteristics of the different types of banks, think about which category might be suitable for the needs of your business. What questions might you ask a prospective bank to help you determine whether or not it's a good fit for your business?

_____
_____
_____
_____

Adam and Alex are two young entrepreneurs from San Diego. Both are seeking outside financing for the first time and have decided to apply for a bank loan in order to help them fund their growing businesses. However, their individual financial needs and expectations differ: Alex is seeking a small loan to help him launch a freelance photography business, while Adam is preparing to expand his existing landscaping business and requires significantly more funding. Alex's long-term financial needs are also much less than Adam's, who's financial needs will most likely increase over time. All of these factors play a part in determining the type of bank that each entrepreneur might consider.

Based on what you learned in Chapter 1, which of the primary bank categories should each entrepreneur consider first? Why would this category be most appropriate for Adam or Alex's individual wants and needs? Furthermore, would you recommend avoiding a specific type of bank based on what each entrepreneur is seeking? Why do you think one category of bank is more appropriate than the others?

DISCUSSION TOPICS FOR ENTREPRENEURS

- Know your strengths & weaknesses: it's important that entrepreneurs understand what they are good at, and more importantly, in what areas they need to improve. By understanding your strengths and weaknesses, you can actively build a network of people that can help you along the way and offset any shortcomings you might have (pg. 19). What are your top three strengths? How about your biggest weakness? What can you do to overcome this weakness?

- Create a Network: one of the first things you will want to do is find an advisor that can work with you and help you from start to finish. As your business grows, you will want to create a professional network of other people that can assist and advise you with challenges and strategies (pg. 21). Who would be on your "short list" of people you could reach out to for advice and wise counsel?

- Don't Hesitate to Ask Questions: take time to prepare before a meeting to understand what will be discussed. It's also a great idea to write down any questions or topics of interest before a meeting so you are ready to discuss them when appropriate (pg. 24). Can you think of a recent meeting where you successfully prepared in this way?

CHAPTER 2: MEET THE BANKING TEAM

INTRODUCTION

In Chapter 2, you were introduced to a few of the primary bank team members with whom you will be working while your loan application is processed. As you learned, there are many different people at most banks and each has specific duties and responsibilities. Think about how the banking team is involved in your loan application and try to come up with a few questions you might ask the bank in a real-life scenario. Remember – effective communication is one of the most important factors in building a successful banking relationship.

LEARNING OBJECTIVES

After reading chapter 2 and completing the review exercises in this unit of the study guide, you will be able to:

- Identify the different team members at a bank
- Describe the role of each team member as it relates to obtaining a bank loan
- Explain the general process of submitting a loan application for approval
- More effectively communicate your wants and needs to a prospective bank

BANKING TEAM MEMBERS

WHO IS INVOLVED IN YOUR LOAN APPROVAL PROCESS?

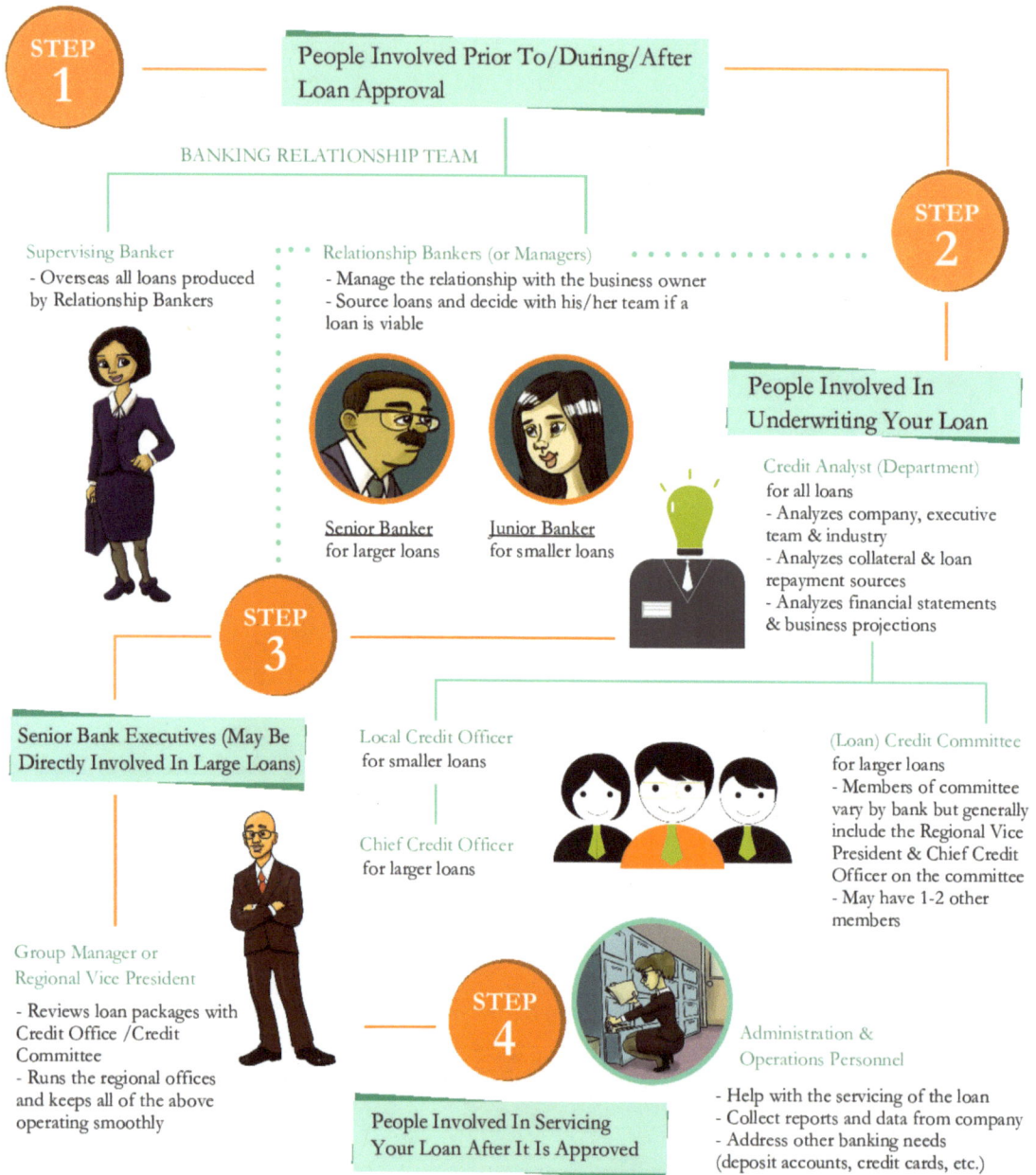

STEP 1

People Involved Prior To/During/After Loan Approval

BANKING RELATIONSHIP TEAM

STEP 2

Supervising Banker
- Overseas all loans produced by Relationship Bankers

Relationship Bankers (or Managers)
- Manage the relationship with the business owner
- Source loans and decide with his/her team if a loan is viable

Senior Banker for larger loans

Junior Banker for smaller loans

People Involved In Underwriting Your Loan

Credit Analyst (Department) for all loans
- Analyzes company, executive team & industry
- Analyzes collateral & loan repayment sources
- Analyzes financial statements & business projections

STEP 3

Senior Bank Executives (May Be Directly Involved In Large Loans)

Local Credit Officer for smaller loans

Chief Credit Officer for larger loans

(Loan) Credit Committee for larger loans
- Members of committee vary by bank but generally include the Regional Vice President & Chief Credit Officer on the committee
- May have 1-2 other members

Group Manager or Regional Vice President

- Reviews loan packages with Credit Office /Credit Committee
- Runs the regional offices and keeps all of the above operating smoothly

STEP 4

People Involved In Servicing Your Loan After It Is Approved

Administration & Operations Personnel

- Help with the servicing of the loan
- Collect reports and data from company
- Address other banking needs (deposit accounts, credit cards, etc.)

Copyright 2020 FIT Advisors, LLC

15

A. VOCABULARY MATCH

Match the term to the correct definition   *Answers*
1. Relationship Banker   1. ____
2. Supervising Banker   2. ____
3. Credit Analyst   3. ____
4. Credit Officer / Credit Committee   4. ____
5. Group Manager / Regional Vice   5. ____
    President

A. Oversees Relationship Bankers and the loans they produce
B. Analyzes the company, executive team, and industry as well as sources of repayment and collateral
C. Manages the primary relationship with the business owner and sources loans for the bank
D. Responsible for the operations of one or more regional offices; Often reviews loan packages with Credit Officer (or Credit Committee)
E. Responsible for reviewing and deciding whether or not to approve a loan

B. TRUE OR FALSE

1. ____ The first person involved in the loan approval process is usually the relationship banker

2. ____ The relationship banker oversees all loans produced by junior bankers

3. ____ A junior banker can usually approve a small loan without getting Chief Credit Officer approval

4. ____ The supervising banker is the person who ultimately reviews and approves/disapproves a loan

5. ____ The regional vice president oversees the bank's regional offices and keeps everything operating smoothly

C. FILL IN THE BLANK

1. The _____ is the first member of the banking team you will meet; they may provide guidance and insights to help you prepare the necessary loan application materials.

2. After you submit your application, it will be analyzed, evaluated, and prepared by the _____, who will make a recommendation and then submit for further review and approval.

3. As your business continues to grow, you may eventually need more _____ or a larger loan.

4. The _____ is the person/team who will ultimately review the loan package and determine whether or not it is approved.

KEY THEMES & CONCEPTS:

- How do you launch your banking relationship – who do you speak to first? Who else should you contact and what would you ask? What do you want to learn in the first meeting, etc.?

- Suppose that you meet with someone at the bank and your first impression is less than ideal (give examples) – how would you address this and what are some of the options available to you?

SHORT ANSWER

1. Imagine that you are going into a new bank for the first time. Think about the following: Who would you talk to first? What would you say to them? What questions would you have?

_____
_____
_____
_____

2. Several people from the banking team will be involved in processing and reviewing your loan application. Describe at least two different employees at the bank and how they are involved in the loan process.

_____
_____
_____
_____

3. Think about who does what for the banking team and come up with a relevant question to ask each of the following members of the banking team:
    o Relationship Banker
    o Credit Analyst
    o Credit Officer

_____
_____
_____
_____

Jennifer started an online business that has been steadily growing for several years. She now believes that she is ready to apply for a bank loan to help fund her business' future growth. Until now, she successfully managed to operate and finance her business using her own personal finances. As such, she has almost no experience with small business banking and has not yet established a business relationship with the bank.

Based on what you learned in Chapter 2, think about the ways in which Jennifer can start a new banking relationship. What should she do first and who should she talk to in order to get started? What kinds of questions might she ask? Consider what you have learned about the bank's expectations and think about how the bank might respond to a small business owner like Jennifer.

DISCUSSION TOPICS FOR ENTREPRENEURS

- Always collect your thoughts and take notes about anything you don't understand so you can review it later with your advisor (pg. 31). Why should you write these down during the meeting or immediately after?

- Come up with an 'elevator pitch' (a 30-second or less brief description of your business) that quickly and concisely explains your business, background, and goals. You will need to memorize this and practice for any new introductions or important meetings (pg. 29). What would you include in your "elevator pitch"?

- Set aside time immediately after any meeting to take notes, draw diagrams, and/or sum up all the important information so you don't forget key points (pg. 34). Can you think of a time where you wish you had taken better notes? How would this have helped you?

CHAPTER 3: BANK LOANS – ADVANTAGES & DISADVANTAGES

INTRODUCTION

In Chapter 3, you became more familiar with commercial bank loans and the associated advantages and disadvantages. As you learned, bank loans are only one of the several financing options available to small businesses. As such, it is important that you familiarize yourself with the benefits, requirements, and general characteristics of commercial bank loans so you can make a more informed decision when the time comes to choose your funding source. As you prepare to complete the following exercises, think about the typical requirements of a bank loan and how a bank loan can impact a company's operating finances.

LEARNING OBJECTIVES

After reading chapter 3 and completing the review exercises in this unit of the study guide, you will be able to:

- Identify various advantages and disadvantages associated with using a bank loan to finance your business
- Determine whether or not you can meet the bank's requirements for bank loans
- Explain how sources of repayment and collateral are tied to the loan process
- Describe how bank loans can impact a business' operating finances (balance sheet, cash-flow, etc.)
- Recognize and assess the risks and potential challenges of using borrowed cash to fund a business
- Assess your funding needs and identify viable loan programs

ADVANTAGES & DISADVANTAGES OF A BANK LOAN

ADVANTAGES

Lower Interest Rates
- Rates can be fixed or variable
- Can lock in low rate and plan payments

Significant Tax Benefits
- Interest is tax-deductible
- Reduces "net cost" of loan even more significantly lowering the cost of the loan.

Various Loan Programs Are Available
- SBA options are excellent
- Can find loan to meet your specific needs

Cheaper to Obtain Than Other Sources of Capital
- Reasonable application fees and on-going costs

Does Not Require Diluting Business Ownership
- As opposed to selling equity

Terms of Use Are Generally Flexible
- Use of loan proceeds are flexible as long as you maintain covenants

DISADVANTAGES

Loan Is Hard To Obtain Unless Business Is Well-Established
- Very challenging for start-up businesses
- Generally require 2 years of profitable operation

Application Process Can Be Burdensome & Time Consuming
- Many forms and documents required

Requires Multiple Sources of Collateral and Repayment
- Bank will require collateral from business and personal guarantees from major owners

Approved Loan Amount Might Be Less Than Desired/Needed
- You may still need additional sources of capital

Loan Repayment Will Affect Cash Balance Of Business
- Principal & interest payments are generally on a set schedule

Debt Increases Leverage & Affects Balance Sheet Ratios
- Increased debt may restrict further borrowings

Applicant Needs Good Credit
- Will need to explain any credit problems

A. Vocabulary Match

Match the term to the correct definition   *Answers*

1. SBA   1. ____
2. SBICs   2. ____
3. Peer-to-peer (P2P) Lending   3. ____
4. Quantitative Traits   4. ____
5. Qualitative Traits   5. ____
6. "Bankable"   6. ____
7. Assets   7. ____
8. Collateral   8. ____
9. Free Cash Flow   9. ____
10. Balance Sheet Ratios   10. ____
11. Leverage   11. ____

A. Describes a business that is financially stable with adequate sources of repayment and sufficient prospects for future success
B. The assets a borrower pledges to a lender to secure approval of a loan. Usually includes things that the business owns, such as real estate, equipment, inventory, and the accounts receivable
C. Privately run firms that loan funds to and sometimes invest in small businesses
D. The cash generated by a business that is available to repay debt and other obligations
E. A relatively recent source of loans through which an individual or financial institution will make loans via a lending portal (such as Lending Club or Prosper.com)
F. Items (tangible and intangible) owned by a person or company and regarded as having value. Used as collateral for loans and obligations to a bank.
G. The use of borrowed money to finance the growth of a company
H. Financial ratios calculated by using financial data from a company's balance sheet
I. Calculable and measurable information such as financials and growth rates
J. A U. S. government agency that provides support to entrepreneurs and small businesses
K. Subjective or abstract aspects of a business that are difficult to measure and calculate or quantify, such as control and leadership, yet are essential to evaluating a company.

B. True or False

1. ____ Most bank financing is available at interest rates that range from mid-single digits to around 10 percent
2. ____ Compared to other debt sources, bank loans are among the cheapest sources of capital available
3. ____ There are no significant tax benefits for borrowing from a bank
4. ____ Unlike some sources of funds, bank loans do not normally require you to dilute your ownership in the business
5. ____ All businesses are bankable
6. ____ Good credit history will help you when you apply for a bank loan

1. Most bank financing is available at interest rates that range from mid-single digits to _____ percent.

2. In comparison to other debt sources, bank loans are one of the _____ sources of _____ to fund your business.

3. _____ may have low 'teaser' rates but generally carry interest rates between 13% and 18% and can go as high as 30%.

4. _____ is a relatively new source of loans where an individual or financial institution will make loans via a lending portal.

5. One benefit to borrowing from a bank is that there are significant _____ because your business can deduct the interest it pays to the bank as a deductible business expense.

6. Entrepreneurs sometimes sell _____ to raise capital, thereby giving up _____ of the company in exchange for cash.

7. With bank loans, you are normally able to retain 100% _____ of your business.

8. Term loans, lines of credit, and loans to help fund large purchase orders and working capital are all available from the _____.

9. Another significant advantage of working with the bank is that you have _____ in how you use the money.

10. Some recent statistics indicate that loan approval percentages are _____.

11. A _____ business is one that is financially stable with adequate _____ and sufficient prospects for future success.

12. The bank will require _____ to provide security for your loan.

13. _____ are privately run firms that loan funds to and sometimes invest in small businesses.

KEY THEMES & CONCEPTS:

- What are the primary benefits of using bank financing to fund your business?

- How do the benefits of bank financing compare to alternative sources of funding?

- What are some of the risks associated with using bank financing to fund a small business?

SHORT ANSWER

1. Review the infographic titled 'Advantages & Disadvantages of a Bank Loan' (pg. 39) and think about which advantages & disadvantages might be particularly important to you. Then identify two bullets from each category and explain why these might be significant when it comes time to apply for the loan.

_____

_____

_____

_____

2. In the last chapter, you learned that ownership and control are important factors to consider when funding your business. In the space below, describe how important ownership and control are to you. Why might you need to consider selling equity in the business to raise cash?

_____

_____

_____

_____

3. The term 'bankable' is used throughout the last chapter. As you now know, not all businesses are bankable. Choose a business to use as an example, then identify and discuss at least two characteristics that make it bankable. Why and how do these traits improve its bankability?

_____

_____

_____

_____

In his spare time, Donovan operates a small plant nursery specializing in exotic tropical fruits. For the past several years, he has been able to operate the business using income from his full-time job. Donovan is passionate about exotic plants and he is considering expanding his nursery to a larger location and operating it full-time. Moving to a larger location would require a moderately sizable bank loan, not to mention other expenses such as the additional cost of hiring employees. Without the income from his full-time job, Donovan isn't sure that he could meet the financial requirements.

Consider what you learned in Chapter 3 and think about the various advantages and disadvantages that Donovan will have to consider before making a decision. Why might it be a worthwhile investment and how could the bank help Donovan to meet his goal? What are some of the potential risks that Donovan will face if he decides to pursue this plan? Is one loan program more viable than others, and if so, why? If you were in Donovan's place, how would you explain and assess the potential long-term financial risks associated with quitting your job in order to run a small business full-time?

Discussion Topics for Entrepreneurs

- An entrepreneur faces many challenges. Stay positive but realistic: consistency and focus are generally more important than accomplishing everything as quickly as possible (pg. 47). Do you know anyone who always seems to handle challenges effortlessly? How do you think they achieve this?

- Always plan for the worst-case scenario; if possible, model what you would need to do and determine whether your business could operate under less than ideal conditions (pg. 51). Describe a time where you overcame a business challenge. What did you do to overcome the challenge?

Chapter 4: Small Business Administration (SBA) Loan Programs

Introduction

In Chapter 4, we explored several loan programs offered by the Small Business Administration (SBA). Like traditional loans, SBA loans have unique requirements, advantages and disadvantages that you should fully analyze and consider before making a decision. As you learned in Chapter 4, in some cases, small business owners with little to no operating history will find that SBA loans are a more viable option than traditional bank loans. As you prepare to complete the following exercises, consider what you have previously learned about traditional commercial bank loans and compare that with what you learned about SBA loan programs.

Learning Objectives

After reading chapter 4 and completing the review exercises in this unit of the study guide, you will be able to:

- Describe how SBA loans differ from traditional commercial bank loans
- Compare and contrast the advantages of using an SBA loan versus a different source of funding
- Describe the unique requirements of SBA loans
- Identify and describe various specialized SBA loan programs (such as the SBA Express Loan program)

SMALL BUSINESS ADMINISTRATION (SBA) LOAN PROGRAMS

ADVANTAGES

Flexible use
Financing is available for almost any business purpose

Large loans amounts available
Over $10 million dollars under some programs

SBA guarantees a percentage of loan
Minimizing risk to lending partner

Flexible repayment terms
Fixed and Variable terms available

Long repayment terms
Up to 25 years are available under some programs

Less collateral required versus a traditional commercial loan

REQUIREMENTS & DISADVANTAGES

SBA offers loans to businesses only
Disaster loans are an exception

Must be a "small" business
There are size, income and net worth requirements

Must be a for-profit business & operating in the United States

Must not be a 'prohibited' business (i.e. - lenders, life insurance companies, MLM companies or any business conducting illegal activity)*

Must not be delinquent on any taxes or other monies owed to the US government

Additional SBA paperwork is required, which may extend approval time

Guarantee fees can be large depending on size of loan

*This list is not all-inclusive. There are other types of prohibited businesses. Check the SBA website for additional details.

A. VOCABULARY MATCH

Match the term to the correct definition   *Answers*

1. Small Business Administration (SBA)   1. ____
2. Prohibited Business   2. ____
3. SBA Express Loan Program   3. ____
4. Military Reservist Economic Injury   4. ____
   Disaster Loan Program
5. Small Business Investment Companies   5. ____
   (SBICs)

A. A streamlined loan program that comes with a highly competitive rate and fairly quick turnaround time

B. Specifically intended for veterans in the military reserves, this program provides extremely low interest loans to help you run the business if you are ever called to an extended period of active duty.

C. Privately owned and managed funds that use their own capital to invest in equity or make loans to small businesses

D. Businesses that are restricted from receiving SBA financing, such as those that lend money, participate in multi-level marketing, or involve gambling or illegal activity

E. A United States government agency that offers financing and loan assistance to small businesses

B. TRUE OR FALSE

1. ____ SBA loans tend to be more flexible than non-SBA loans

2. ____ Because the government backs a percentage of the loan, there is greater risk for the funding bank if you don't repay the loan

3. ____ You cannot borrow significant amounts of money (greater than $500,000) with an SBA loan

4. ____ SBA programs generally require less collateral than a traditional commercial loan

5. ____ SBA loans are available to both businesses and individuals

6. ____ In order to qualify for an SBA loan, your company must be classified as a small business

7. ____ SBA loans are only available to businesses operating in the United States

8. ____ Unlike other SBA loan programs, the SBA Express Loans are not very flexible in terms of loan usage

9. ____ The SBA is licensed and regulated by the SBIC

10. ____ SBICs can provide technical assistance to small businesses and entrepreneurs, usually at little to no cost

1. One significant advantage to an SBA loan is its _____ since financing is available for just about any valid business purpose.

2. Because the government _____ a percentage of the loans, there is less risk to the funding bank.

3. SBA loans have a flexible _____ that can be as long as 7 to 25 years for some loan programs.

4. SBA programs generally require less _____ than a traditional commercial loan, making more businesses eligible.

5. The SBA offers loans only to _____, so the eligibility requirements are based on the business and not the individual.

6. The SBA will deny any loan request if you are delinquent on any _____ you owe to the U.S. government.

7. The SBA's _____ program comes with a highly competitive rate and fairly quick turnaround time.

8. Military veterans can take advantage of the _____ program, which provides extremely low interest loans to help run the business if said veteran is ever called to an extended period of active duty.

9. _____ are privately owned and managed funds that use their own capital to invest in _____ or make loans to small businesses.

10. Businesses categorized as _____ are ones that generate social, environmental, and economic returns in addition to profits.

CORE CONCEPT REVIEW

KEY THEMES & CONCEPTS:

- How do Small Business Administration (SBA) loan programs differ from traditional bank loans?

- What are some of the primary advantages of using SBA loan financing instead of traditional bank financing? What are some of the primary disadvantages?

- What types of entrepreneurs might benefit from using an SBA loan instead of a bank loan to finance their small business? Why might someone want to choose a bank loan instead of an SBA loan and why?

1. Review the infographic titled 'Small Business Administration (SBA) Loan Programs' (pg. 57) and think about which advantages & disadvantages might be particularly important to you. Then identify two bullets from each and explain why these might be significant when it comes time to apply for the loan.

    _____
    _____
    _____
    _____
    _____
    _____
    _____

2. The SBA offers many different loan programs, some of which are specialized and subject to certain requirements. Review the infographic titled 'SBA Loan Programs' (pg. 61) and identify any programs for which your business might qualify.

    _____
    _____
    _____
    _____
    _____
    _____
    _____

3. In addition to its unique loan programs, the SBA offers other services to entrepreneurs and small businesses. Aside from its loan programs, describe a few additional services that the SBA provides that might be useful to you and your business?

    _____
    _____
    _____
    _____
    _____
    _____

In the previous chapter, we met a green-thumbed entrepreneur named Donovan. If you recall, Donovan is considering a bank loan in order to expand his part-time exotic fruit nursery into a full-time operation, complete with larger location and a few employees. After speaking with Alan, his close friend and financial advisor, Donovan decided to check out the Small Business Administration (SBA) to see if they offer any specific loan programs that might be a better fit than a traditional bank loan. He is especially interested in the SBA Express Loan Program, as well as the SBA's Microloan programs.

Think about the various characteristics and advantages/disadvantages of SBA loan programs and compare these to what you have learned about traditional bank loans. Given Donovan's limited finances and required loan amount, do you think the SBA's loan programs would be a better fit for Donovan's needs compared to a bank loan? If you were in his position, which would you choose and why? Is the SBA Express Loan Program Donovan's best option or is there a different loan type/program that you would recommend more? What led you to this conclusion?

DISCUSSION TOPICS FOR ENTREPRENEURS

- Take time to research unfamiliar topics that you know will be covered during a meeting. This will help you better comprehend what is being said at the time of the meeting (pg. 61). Can you think of a time where you would have been completely unfamiliar with a topic if you had not done your research in advance?

- Whenever possible, plan ahead for meetings and arrive at least 15 minutes early to give yourself time to collect your thoughts and relax (pg. 61). Are you habitually late to everything, or normally prompt and on time? How does this affect those you work with?

- When applying for a business loan, be aware of any personal or business characteristics (military veteran, minority status, socio-economic background, etc.) that may qualify you for specialized SBA loan programs or government grants (pg. 65). Do you know if you are eligible for any special government lending programs or grants? If so, how might you leverage this status to grow your business?

UNIT REVIEW TEST #1: CH. 1 – 4

A. VOCABULARY MATCH

Match the term to the correct definition   *Answers*

1. Relationship Banker   1. ____
2. Supervising Banker   2. ____
3. Credit Analyst   3. ____
4. Credit Officer / Credit Committee   4. ____
5. Small Business Administration (SBA)   5. ____
6. Small Business Investment Company (SBIC)   6. ____
7. Bankable   7. ____
8. Assets   8. ____
9. Collateral   9. ____
10. Free Cash Flow   10. ____
11. Leverage   11. ____

A. A United States government agency that provides support to entrepreneurs and small businesses
B. Property owned by a person or company, regarded as having value and available to meet debts, commitments, or legacies
C. Refers to a business that is financially stable with adequate sources of repayment and sufficient prospects for future success
D. The cash generated by a business that is available to repay debt and other obligations
E. Responsible for reviewing and deciding whether or not to approve a loan
F. Manages the relationship with the business owner and sources potential loans
G. The use of borrowed money to finance the growth of a company
H. Analyzes the company, executive team, and industry as well as sources of repayment and collateral
I. Privately owned and managed funds that use their own capital to invest in equity or make loans to small businesses
J. The assets a borrower pledges to a lender to secure approval of a loan. Usually includes things that the business owns, such as real estate, equipment, inventory, and the accounts receivable
K. Oversees all loans produced by Relationship Bankers

B. TRUE OR FALSE

1. ___ The four primary categories of banks are community banks, regional banks, multinational banks, and international banks

2. ___ Regional banks are the smallest type of bank in terms of assets under management and number of retail branches

3. ___ Small banks and large banks usually offer the same ancillary bank services

4. ___ Banks and credit unions are the same thing

5. ___ Credit unions have historically focused more on consumer loans and less on business lending

6. ___ The first person involved in the loan approval process is usually the relationship banker

7. ___ The supervising banker is normally the person who ultimately reviews and approves or disapproves your loan

8. ___ Banks will never lend to a college student, even if they operate a profitable business because they may be under 21 years of age

9. ___ Compared to other debt sources, bank loans are among the cheapest sources of capital available

10. ___ Unlike some sources of funds, bank loans do not normally require you to dilute your ownership in the business

11. ___ One significant disadvantage to borrowing from the bank is that you don't have much flexibility in how you can use the money

12. ___ All businesses are bankable

13. ___ SBA loans are known for their flexibility

14. ___ SBA programs generally require less collateral than a traditional commercial loan

15. ___ In order to qualify for an SBA loan, you must be classified as a small business

16. ___ SBA loans are only available to businesses operating in the United States

17. ___ Unlike other SBA loan programs, the SBA Express Loans are not very flexible in terms of loan usage

18. ___ SBICs can provide technical assistance to small businesses and entrepreneurs, usually at little to no cost

C. FILL IN THE BLANK / MULTIPLE CHOICE

1. The smallest categories of banks in terms of both assets under management and number of retail branches are _____, followed by _____.
    a. Local Community Banks; Regional Domestic Banks
    b. Credit Unions; Local Community Banks
    c. Local Community Banks; Multinational Banks
    d. Local Community Banks; Credit Unions

2. In addition to commercial loans, most banks offer many _____ such as cash management and retirement planning services.
    a. Consulting Services
    b. Fiscal Management Services
    c. Ancillary Services
    d. 401K Plans

3. Credit Unions tend to be more accommodating and family-like since they are _____.
    a. Privately-Owned
    b. Member-Owned
    c. Government-Owned
    d. Owned by large, privately-funded Venture Capital Funds

4. The _____ is the first member of the banking team you will meet; their job is to help you prepare the necessary loan application materials.
    a. Relationship Banker
    b. Supervising Banker
    c. Credit Officer
    d. Janitor

5. After you submit your application, it will be analyzed, evaluated, and prepared by the _____, who will make a recommendation and then submit for further review and approval.
    a. Credit Officer
    b. Relationship Banker
    c. Chief Executive Officer (CEO)
    d. Credit Analysts

6. The _____ is the person that will ultimately review the loan package and determine whether or not it is approved.
    a. Relationship Banker
    b. Relationship Counseling Banker
    c. Credit Officer
    d. Head Honcho / Big Cheese

7. In comparison to other debt sources, bank loans are generally one of the _____ sources of _____ to fund your business.
    a. Most Flexible; Equity
    b. Cheapest; Capital
    c. Most Time-Consuming; Capital
    d. Easiest; Equity

8. _____ is a relatively new source of loans where an individual or financial institution will make loans via a lending portal.
    a. e-Commerce
    b. Crowdfunding
    c. Loansharking
    d. Peer-to-Peer (P2P) Lending

9. One benefit to borrowing from a bank is the significant _____ because your business can deduct the interest it pays to bank as a business tax write-off.
    a. Tax Benefit
    b. Capital
    c. Control & Ownership
    d. Bankability

10. Entrepreneurs sometimes sell _____ to raise capital, thereby giving up some _____ of the company in exchange for cash.
    a. Baked goods; refreshments
    b. Equity; Ownership & Control
    c. Hard Money Loans; Equity
    d. Control & Ownership; Assets

11. Another significant advantage of working with a bank is that you have _____ in how you use the money.
    a. Absolutely no input
    b. Ownership
    c. Influence
    d. Flexibility

12. Failure to adequately prepare the _____ and the _____ is one of the biggest reasons that loans fail to get approved.
    a. Collateral; Personal Guarantees
    b. Loan Application; Proxy Statements
    c. Pro-Forma Projections; Business Plan
    d. Financial History; Financial Projections

13. A _____ business is one that is financially stable with adequate _____ and sufficient prospects for future success.
    a. Established; Revenue
    b. Bankable; Sources of Repayment
    c. Growing; Assets
    d. Small; Collateral

14. The bank will require _____ to provide security for your loan.
    a. Collateral
    b. Legal Documentation
    c. Your Firstborn Child
    d. Pro Forma Projections

15. _____ are privately run firms that loan funds to, and sometimes invest in, small businesses.
    a. OPMs
    b. SBICs
    c. SBAs
    d. BBBs

16. One significant advantage to an SBA loan is its _____ since financing is available for just about any valid business purpose.
    a. Control
    b. Ownership
    c. Changeability
    d. Flexibility

17. The SBA's _____ program comes with a highly competitive rate and fairly quick turnaround time.
    a. Express Loan
    b. Fast Cash
    c. Franchise Startup Loan
    d. Small Business Investment Loan

18. Military veterans can take advantage of the _____ program, which provides extremely low interest loans to help run the business if said veteran is ever called to an extended period of active duty.
    a. Military Reservist Economic Injury Disaster Loan
    b. Veteran Entrepreneurship Investment Loan
    c. Wounded Warriors
    d. SBA Express Loan

19. Your _____ affects how much capacity, if any, your business has to borrow additional funds.
    a. Executive team's social media profiles
    b. Physical Office Location
    c. Leverage, or existing debt load
    d. Company Website

20. Businesses categorized as _____ are ones that generate social, environmental, and economic returns in addition to profits.
    a. Social Welfare
    b. Impact Investments
    c. Non-Profit Organizations
    d. Community Service Organizations

UNIT REVIEW TEST #1 ANSWER SHEET

A. VOCABULARY MATCH

1. _____
2. _____
3. _____
4. _____
5. _____
6. _____

7. _____
8. _____
9. _____
10. _____
11. _____

B. TRUE OR FALSE

1. _____
2. _____
3. _____
4. _____
5. _____
6. _____
7. _____
8. _____
9. _____

10. _____
11. _____
12. _____
13. _____
14. _____
15. _____
16. _____
17. _____
18. _____

C. MULTIPLE CHOICE

1. _____
2. _____
3. _____
4. _____
5. _____
6. _____
7. _____
8. _____
9. _____
10. _____

11. _____
12. _____
13. _____
14. _____
15. _____
16. _____
17. _____
18. _____
19. _____
20. _____

UNIT #2

CH. 5 – CH. 7

Ch. 5: Basics of Bank Lending and the Underwriting Process
Understanding the Underwriting Process | The Five Cs of Underwriting | Financial Considerations

Ch. 6: Applying for the Loan – Personal Documents Required
Preparing the Documents | Understanding the Bank's Rationale | Helpful Hints

Ch. 7: Applying for the Loan – Business Documents Required
Understanding Personal vs. Business Documentation | What to Prepare | Key Considerations & Cautions

CHAPTER 5: BASICS OF BANK LENDING AND THE UNDERWRITING PROCESS

INTRODUCTION

Welcome to Unit 2 of the Approved! Study Guide and Workbook. Over the past four chapters, you have become more familiar with the process of selecting a bank and loan. As we begin Unit 2, you will further explore the process of applying for a bank loan.

In Chapter 5, you learned about underwriting, the process used by the bank to evaluate a prospective borrower and the risk of lending to them. Think about the steps and criteria used during the underwriting process and how these apply to you and your business. Likewise, consider the strategies you can potentially use to demonstrate your credibility and likelihood of repaying the loan. These will all be important as you continue your loan application process.

LEARNING OBJECTIVES

After reading chapter 5 and completing the review exercises in this unit of the study guide, you will be able to:

- Explain what the underwriting process is and how the bank uses it to determine which loans are approved
- Describe the five steps of the underwriting process and the requirements of each step
- Assess your potential sources of repayment and collateral
- Define and differentiate between various financial measurements related to your business' profitability and leverage

HOW A BANK UNDERWRITES YOUR LOAN

"THE UNDERWRITING 5 X 5"

THE BANKING TEAM UNDERTAKES 5 MAJOR STEPS:

1 Evaluates Your Business (Historical & Projected)

Review The Qualifications Of Your Executive Team

Analyze Your Businesses Historical Performance

Analyze The Industry In Which Your Business Operates

2 Evaluates Key Risks Associated With Your Business

Are There Any Troubling Industry Trends?

Is Your Executive Team Experienced In The Key Areas?

Are Your Business Financials Degrading?

3 Determines Sources of Repayment

Is Cash Flow Of Business Adequate To Repay Loan?

Can Business Provide Sufficient Collateral?

Are Personal Guarantees Of Owners Credible?

4 Conducts a Financial Analysis (Income Statement/Balance Sheet /Cash Flow/Financial Ratios)

Review Your Businesses Historical Performance

Review Your Businesses Projections For Next 3-5 Years

Test Loan Covenants For Various Scenarios

5 Reviews & Prepares Loan Package

Credit Committee Reviews Summary Of Steps 1-4

Approves Loan & Prepares Loan Documents For Execution

COLLATERAL

What Assets (Accounts Receivable, Real Estate, Equipment, Etc.) Do You And Your Business Have?

CHARACTER

How Trustworthy Are You & What Experience Do You Have That Will Make The Business Successful?

During These 5 Steps, The Bank Analyzes **The 5 C's** Of Business Loan Qualification

CAPACITY

How Much Can Your Business Afford To Repay (Based On Cash Flow)?

CAPITAL

How Much Is Your Business Worth?

CONDITIONS

Will External Conditions Related To Customers, Competitors Or The Economy Affect Your Business?

Chapter 5 Exercises

A. Vocabulary Match

Match the term to the correct definition

		Answers
1.	Underwriting	1. ____
2.	Loan Loss Rate	2. ____
3.	Real Property	3. ____
4.	"The 5 Cs": capacity, capital, conditions, collateral, and character	4. ____
5.	Sources of Repayment	5. ____
6.	Unsecured Loans	6. ____
7.	Collateral	7. ____
8.	Blanket Lien	8. ____
9.	Assignment of Claims	9. ____
10.	Income Statement	10. ____
11.	Balance Sheet	11. ____
12.	Cash-Flow Statement	12. ____

A. The five primary items that the bank evaluates as they relate to you and your business

B. A financial statement that measures a company's financial performance (sales, cost of sales, expenses, and any profit/loss) during a specific measurement period

C. Loans that do not require specific collateral to support the loan; tend to be very costly because money is borrowed purely on your personal creditworthiness

D. Sources of funds that the bank expects the business to use to repay any outstanding indebtedness

E. A security interest placed by a bank on some or all of a company's assets

F. The process by which banks analyze, evaluate and document a loan prior to lending the funds.

G. A financial statement that provides a snapshot of the financial health of a company; it highlights the assets, liabilities, and equity of the business

H. Actual land and any structure built upon it

I. A document filed by a bank (the *assignee*) to transfer the right to payments payable to a company (the *assignor*); often associated with payments from the US government

J. The percentage of loans that do not get repaid to the bank

K. Provides data regarding cash inflows a company receives or pays from its operations, investing activities, and financing sources during a given measurement period

L. Any asset that a borrower pledges to a lender in order to secure approval of a loan

B. True or False

1. ___ All banks follow an underwriting process to evaluate a prospective borrower and the risk of loaning them money

2. ___ Banks must generally achieve a loan loss rate of less than 2%

3. ___ Real Property is anything you personally own

4. ___ The '5 C's of Underwriting' are *capacity, capital, conditions, collateral,* and *collaboration*

5. ___ When underwriting a loan, the bank must always determine sources of repayment

6. ___ The bank will analyze both the company and the industry in which it operates

7. ___ Sources of repayment and collateral are the same thing

8. ___ Most banks require only one source of repayment

9. ___ The three most important financial statements the bank uses are the income statement, the balance sheet, and the cash-flow statement

C. Fill in the Blank

1. All banks follow an _____ to evaluate the risk of loaning to a borrower.

2. Stephen Covey is quoted as saying, "Seek first to _____, then to be _____."

3. A bank has to underwrite its loans stringently enough to achieve a _____ of less than _____ percent.

4. The 5 C's of underwriting are _____, _____, _____, _____, and _____.

5. One of the first things the bank will review is the _____ information on you and your company.

6. When evaluating the business background, the bank will look at you and your _____ and then perform an analysis of both the _____ and the _____.

7. _____ are normally related to items that the bank discovered during the background review and can include things like potential risks and problematic industry trends.

8. Most loans will require multiple _____ and _____ to support the loan.

9. _____ loans are a type of secured loan backed by the assets of the business.

10. Banks will sometimes file an _____, which requires payments be made directly to a specified account that can be taken over by the bank if necessary.

11. The _____ is the one the bank expects will be used to repay the loan while the _____ is normally the assets or collateral that are easiest for the bank to seize and sell.

12. In most cases, a bank is going to require an additional or tertiary source of repayment called a _____.

13. According to the text, the three most important financial statements used for the financial analysis are the _____, the _____, and the _____.

KEY THEMES & CONCEPTS:

- What is the Underwriting Process and how is it used to evaluate potential loan applications?

- What is 'The Underwriting 5x5' and what are the five major steps within it?

- Which of the underwriting process' five steps might present potential obstacles or challenges for some entrepreneurs?

SHORT ANSWER

1. Review the five steps covered by the bank during the underwriting process (pg. 69-70) and briefly describe how the bank completes each of the five steps.

_____

_____

_____

_____

2. Think about what the bank looks for when underwriting a new loan. How might you be able to improve your chances of success during the underwriting process?

_____

_____

_____

_____

3. A bank uses the underwriting process to identify and gauge how much risk there is in lending to a particular business. Consider any key risks associated with your business and identify which risks might require additional explanation. How would you explain these risks to the bank?

_____

_____

_____

_____

4. Sources of repayment are among the most important factors the bank considers during the underwriting process. Describe any assets you own that could be declared as a source of repayment or collateral. Identify at least one primary and one secondary source of repayment.

_____

_____

_____

_____

Several years ago, Jessie inherited a significant sum of money from her grandfather. His instructions were to deposit half into a long-term savings account and use the remaining amount to expand her small online cosmetics business. Thanks to a series of smart investments over the past several years, her business has grown from a small side project to a thriving online business. Using some of the money she inherited from her grandfather, Jessie was able to invest in several key pieces of machinery that helped her to triple production and expand her existing product line. Most recently, thanks to several glowing endorsements from established beauty experts and a full-length feature in Beauty Trends Magazine, Jessie is barely able to keep up with the customer demand.

Jessie is considering a bank loan to help finance a small brick-and-mortar store located in a trendy mall close to her home, which she suspects will provide a steady flow of customers within her demographic. She knows that opening a physical location will be much more expensive than operating an exclusively online business and it is likely that she will need to hire several employees and possibly even invest in new machinery to keep up with demand. After considering the various options, Jessie has decided to apply for a bank loan that she will use to fund the initial launch of the brick-and-mortar store as well as hiring new employees and purchasing any necessary equipment.

Part 1: Sources of Repayment & Collateral

As you learned in Chapter 5, a key part of the underwriting process is determining sources of repayment and collateral. Given the loan size that Jessie is seeking, it is very likely that she will need to provide multiple sources of repayment to collateralize the loan. Based on the above information, what sources of repayment might Jessie use to collateralize the loan? Remember that sources of repayment can include both personal finances as well as business assets like machinery and product stock. Which of Jessie's sources of repayment are considered business assets and which are personal sources?

Part 2: Evaluating Key Risks

Bank loans come with many risks that can affect not just the business but, more importantly, the business owner and his or her personal finances and security. As such, it is important to fully understand and evaluate all potential risks before making a final decision. Based on what you know about the risks of using bank loans, think about the specific risks that Jessie must consider. What are the primary risks that she faces and what ways can she address or avoid these? What aspects of Jessie's business might concern the bank?

DISCUSSION TOPICS FOR ENTREPRENEURS

- Know your audience: think about who they are and what they want or need to see to most effectively get your message communicated to them (pg. 70). Can you think of a recent time where you were particularly effective in communicating your message because you truly understood the perspective of your audience/listener?
- Put yourself in the position of a banker: This will help you demonstrate to the bank that you understand the concerns they have and, more important, that you understand how to address them (pg. 75). What would concern you most if you were lending to your business? Draft a list of potential concerns and prepare answers for the most significant issues.

CHAPTER 6: APPLYING FOR THE LOAN – PERSONAL DOCUMENTS REQUIRED

INTRODUCTION

As you have probably realized, your personal finances may affect your ability to obtain a bank loan in the same way as your business finances. The bank will require you to submit documentation for both the business and yourself to evaluate your creditworthiness. In Chapter 6, you learned about the importance of understanding the required personal financial documents and which documents the bank expects you to submit. Consider the ways in which these documents are critically analyzed to determine the potential for the approval of a loan request. Pay close attention to the way the bank often requests similar documents and take note of any documents you need to prepare.

LEARNING OBJECTIVES

After reading chapter 6 and completing the review exercises in this unit of the study guide, you will be able to:

- Identify the personal documents required for the loan application package
- Compare and contrast the two primary types of small business loans
- Understand how to review and prepare the required personal documents
- Explain the bank's rationale for requesting each specific document

PERSONAL INFORMATION
REQUIRED FOR BANK LOAN

Personal Tax Returns	Form 4506 — Request for Personal Tax Transcript	SBA Form 1919 — SBA Borrower Information Form (For SBA Loans Only)	PFS — Personal Financial Statement	Other Required Documents (Business owner's resume, recent pay stubs, etc.)
WHAT? Provide complete copies of two years of your personal tax returns – generally form 1040 and associated schedules.	**WHAT?** This document allows the bank to request a copy of your tax returns directly from the IRS.	**WHAT?** This document requests detailed information about the borrower and other associates of the business.	**WHAT?** This document requests financial data about the business owner. It covers assets, liabilities, income sources and debts; including private debts not listed on your credit report.	**WHAT?** The additional information requested varies by lender; however, generally includes documents used to provide more background about the borrower (i.e. the borrower's resume/profile) or substantiate other data provided (i.e. the pay-stub provides proof of income).
WHY? The bank uses these to validate your personal income and business income/loss.	**WHY?** The bank may use this to order a tax return from the IRS to validate the completeness of the tax returns you have provided.	**WHY?** This is a document required for all SBA guaranteed loans. It required you to certify several things related to the creditworthiness of the borrower(s), the use of the loan proceeds, type of business activity your business performs and any affiliations you have with the SBA or related entities.	**WHY?** The document provides a significant amount of information regarding your financial position, and therefore, your ability to repay the loan. The PFS allows the bank's underwriting team to evaluate your financial position as well as the strength of your personal guarantee.	**WHY?** These documents help support the credit-worthiness of the borrower which can strengthen the underwriting package and improve chances of loan approval.
HELPFUL HINTS: Be prepared to discuss any extra-ordinary or unique items, especially any large losses or gains.	**HELPFUL HINTS:** If married, your spouse will generally be required to sign as well.	**HELPFUL HINTS:** This is a government document. Make sure you fully understand what you are certifying and answer all items truthfully.	**HELPFUL HINTS:** Be prepared to show proof for all income sources and accounts to validate information that you include in your PFS.	**HELPFUL HINTS:** Provide information that will improve your chances of loan approval or explain potentially derogatory or misleading information included in other documents. Include your resume alongside bios of your key executives and any notable advisors.

NOTES FOR ALL DOCUMENTS:
1. Make sure all information requested is provided. If you provide misleading information about income or fail to include information about current debts, it may jeopardize your loan approval or cause a delay in your loan processing while they further scrutinize all information you have provided.
2. If you have questions related to any specific form or document request, make sure to ask your banker or the SBA program office.

Copyright 2020 FIT Advisors, LLC

A. VOCABULARY MATCH

Match the term to the correct definition   *Answers*

1. Fixed or Term Loan   1. ____
2. Revolving Line of Credit   2. ____
3. Amortization Period   3. ____
4. Personal Financial Statement (PFS)   4. ____
5. SBA Form 1919   5. ____

A. Also known as a revolver, it is a line of credit set at an agreed upon limit which the business can draw from when funds are needed, up to the pre-approved limit
B. The time over which you are required to repay the loan
C. A loan from a bank for a specific amount that has a specified repayment schedule
D. This document requests representations and warranties related to the creditworthiness of the borrower(s), the planned use of loan proceeds, business activities, affiliations, and other related topics
E. This document covers assets, liabilities, income sources and debts, including private debts

B. TRUE OR FALSE

1. ___   The two primary types of small business loans are a *term loan* and a *revolving line of credit*

2. ___   A term loan lets you borrow funds, pay them back, then borrow them again

3. ___   The amortization period is the time you have to repay the loan

4. ___   Most banks request similar items when it comes to personal documentation, although they may use bank-specific forms

5. ___   A revolving line of credit does not have a pre-defined limit and can be drawn upon as needed so long as everything is paid back within a pre-defined period

C. FILL IN THE BLANK

1. The _____ is an institution that provides assistance and guidance to small businesses, such as help navigating the loan process.
2. There are two primary types of loans for small businesses: _____ and _____.
3. A _____ lets you borrow funds, pay them back, and then borrow them again.
4. In most cases, small business loans have _____ somewhere between two and five years.
5. A _____ is generally _____, meaning that the interest rate can be set at a fixed rate for a certain period of time.

_____

SHORT ANSWER

1. As you now know, there are two primary types of loans for small business: fixed term loans and revolving lines of credit. Describe the main differences between the two types of loans. Why might a small business choose one over the other? If you had to choose between them, which would you pick and why?

_____
_____
_____
_____

2. As you review the required personal documents described in Ch. 6, think about the real-life process of compiling and submitting loan documents. Which documents might present challenges or require additional explanation? How would you address these issues?

_____
_____
_____
_____

DISCUSSION TOPICS FOR ENTREPRENEURS

- Stay organized: as you apply for a loan, always use checklists and labels to keep everything neatly organized (pg. 86). Are there any checklists that you currently use effectively? What makes them work so well for you?

- Record meetings: if permitted, record all important meetings using a small recorder device or even your phone using your favorite voice recording app (check out Evernote, Things, and Wunderlist for some useful task management apps that feature excellent voice recognition capabilities so you can focus on speaking or listening instead of taking notes and hoping you caught the most important material. By using a recording device during important presentations, meetings, and discussions, you can free your mind to engage exclusively with the topic at hand. You can then transcribe the recording later (pg. 87). How familiar were you with modern recording technology and capacity? Have you used audio or video to record meetings in the past? If so, how did this help you after the meeting?

- Take advantage of local resources: many cities are home to numerous resources for helping small businesses, such as a local SBA office or a SBICs. Don't hesitate to take advantage of what they offer (pg. 88). Have you visited your local SBA office? If so, what was the most beneficial part of your visit?

CHAPTER 7: APPLYING FOR THE LOAN – BUSINESS INFORMATION REQUIRED

INTRODUCTION

Chapter 6 explored the required personal loan documents required for a business loan. In Chapter 7, we discussed the required business documents along with the bank's rationale for requesting them. As you know, it is important to understand how these documents are critically analyzed and cross-referenced by the bank to identify any discrepancies. Think about what you can do to ensure that the provided information is consistent and accurate.

LEARNING OBJECTIVES

After reading chapter 7 and completing the review exercises in this unit of the study guide, you will be able to:

- Identify the business documentation required for the loan application package
- Compare and contrast how the business requirements differ from the personal requirements
- Differentiate between historical financial statements and pro-forma projections
- Understand how to review and prepare the required business documentation / financial statements
- Explain the bank's rationale for requesting each specific document

BUSINESS INFORMATION
REQUIRED FOR BANK LOAN – PART 1

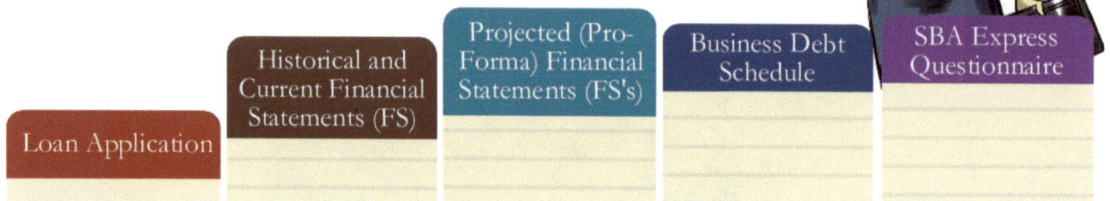

Loan Application

WHAT?
The document is the starting point for all loans and requests information about the business, the owners and the size and type of loan desired.

WHY?
The document is used to gather required information to start the loan application and review process.

HELPFUL HINTS:
Much of the data requested here will be requested in multiple places and on multiple forms, so make sure that the data and answers are consistent across all of them.

Historical and Current Financial Statements (FS)

WHAT?
Include historical & current income statements & current balance sheet. Information related to the ownership & capital structure may be requested.

WHY?
The historical FS's provide the bank a snapshot into the past growth and cyclicality of your business.

HELPFUL HINTS:
The level of detail of financial statements requested will depend on the size of the requested loan and the complexity of your business. Smaller loans may not require any historical financial statements at all.
● Don't create additional historical financial statements if they aren't required by the bank.
● Ask if the business tax returns alone will be sufficient for underwriting purposes.

Projected (Pro-Forma) Financial Statements (FS's)

WHAT?
Include 3 years of projected income statements and balance sheets. The bank may also require cash flow statements to understand how and where the loan proceeds will be used.

WHY?
The projected FS's provide the bank insight into your growth, profitability and ability to repay the loan. The projections for a rapidly-growing business will also provide insight into expected cash use to fund working capital.

HELPFUL HINTS:
The required FS projections will depend greatly on the size of the requested loan and the complexity of the business.
● Before you create extensive projections, ask the bank what they need.

Business Debt Schedule

WHAT?
The document requests detailed information about your businesses loan, lease and other periodic payments.

WHY?
As part of the underwriting process, the ability of the borrower to repay all current & future liabilities are analyzed. The total repayment amounts will also be used to model loan covenants.

HELPFUL HINTS:
Make sure that you fully understand and have analyzed your current and expected debt and your businesses ability to make all required payments. If you are a sole proprietor, make sure you have properly segregated (or have otherwise accounted for) any personal debt.

SBA Express Questionnaire

WHAT?
The document requests details about your business and its owners as well as use of the loan proceeds and existing debt to be repaid with the new loan.

WHY?
This document provides additional information required to evaluate and underwrite the loan.

HELPFUL HINTS:
The "use of loan proceeds" falls into potential "buckets" like
1) Business Purchase
2) Real Estate acquisition
3) Machinery/Equipment
4) Working Capital
5) Debt Refinance or
6) Other

NOTES FOR ALL DOCUMENTS:
1. Make sure all information requested is provided. If you provide misleading information about income or fail to include information about current debts, it may jeopardize your loan approval or cause a delay in your loan processing while they further scrutinize all information you have provided.
2. If you have questions related to any specific form or document request, make sure to ask your banker or the SBA program office.

BUSINESS INFORMATION
REQUIRED FOR BANK LOAN - PART 2

EIN Confirmation Letter from the IRS

Business Tax Returns

Formation & Other Organizational Documents

Business Plan

WHAT?

This is a one-page document that provides the name of your business, the Employer Identification Number (EIN) and the date it was granted. It also provides, the expected type of federal tax return, and information regarding potential payroll tax filings.

WHY?

The bank may use this to validate other information you have provided in the loan application, including a review of the tax forms the IRS indicates you should be filing.

HELPFUL HINTS:

If your business does not have employees other than yourself and spouse, you may not be required to have an EIN.

WHAT?

These include the tax returns filed by your business, including all schedules.

WHY?

The bank uses these for multiple purposes, including validating the businesses income, assets and associated depreciation schedules. They will also evaluate any potential undisclosed tax liabilities that may affect future cash flow.

HELPFUL HINTS:

If there are any extra-ordinary or unique items present, you should be prepared to discuss them. In fact, if you know they may be a problem, such as a large business loss, you should provide details along with the tax returns.

WHAT?

Corporations require a certificate of incorporation & bylaws. Limited liability company's (LLC's), sole proprietorships or partnerships will have different documents (Operating Agreements and /or Partnership Agreements).

WHY?

These documents demonstrate that company was properly formed. For corporations, the bylaws and resolutions also lay out who is authorized to enter into contractual agreements (such as a bank loan).

HELPFUL HINTS:

The bank will request a Certificate of Good Standing from the state where you are located (& the state of incorporation if they are different) to ensure the business is current with all taxes and required filings.

WHAT?

The business plan covers the history of the business, the executive team, a description of the products & services offered, an analysis of competitors, sales and marketing plans and financials.

WHY?

A well-prepared business plan demonstrates that the executives have properly researched all aspects of their business & adds a huge amount of credibility during the underwriting process.

HELPFUL HINTS:

A well-done business plan establishes credibility but a poorly written one can do the exact opposite.
- Make sure that the executive summary is excellent & covers all key points.
- Make the business plan concise and easily readable.

NOTES FOR ALL DOCUMENTS:

1. Make sure all information requested is provided. If you provide misleading information about income or fail to include information about current debts, it may jeopardize your loan approval or cause a delay in your loan processing while they further scrutinize all information you have provided.
2. If you have questions related to any specific form or document request, make sure to ask your banker or the SBA program office.

A. VOCABULARY MATCH

Match the term to the correct definition   *Answers*

1. Loan Application   1. _____
2. Historical Financial Statements   2. _____
3. Projected/Pro-Forma Financial   3. _____
   Statements   4. _____
4. Income Statements   5. _____
5. Balance Sheets   6. _____
6. Business Debt Schedule   7. _____
7. SBA Express Questionnaire   8. _____
8. EIN Confirmation Letter   9. _____
9. Business Tax Returns   10. _____
10. Company Formation Documents /
    Certificates of Good Standing   11. _____
11. Business Plan

A. This document requests details about your business and its owners, as well as information about the use of the loan proceeds and any existing debt to be repaid with your new SBA loan

B. This document, if properly done, is an excellent summary of all aspects of the business; it covers a variety of topics including the business' history, management team, product/service offerings, and financials.

C. Also known as the Profit and Loss Statement, this financial statement measures a company's financial performance (sales, cost of sales, expenses, and profits or losses) during a specific measurement period

D. These documents demonstrate that a company was properly formed and remains in good standing, and further support the legal name, location, and other information regarding the business

E. These projections offer the bank insight into the expected growth of your business and your ability to repay the loan

F. This document is the starting point for all loans and is used to gather information required to start the loan application and review process

G. Also known as the Statement of Financial Position, this document provides a snapshot of the financial health of a company on a particular date

H. This document requires detailed information about all current loans, leases, and other large periodic bills for which your business is responsible

I. A document that provides the name of your business, the Employer Identification Number (EIN), and the date it was granted

J. These financial statements provide the bank with a snapshot into the past growth, financial stability, and cyclicality of your business

K. Used by the bank to validate a business' income, assets, and depreciation schedules and any potential undisclosed tax liabilities

1. ___ Most of the data requested in the loan application packet will be requested in multiple places and on several forms

2. ___ Historical Financial Statements provide a snapshot into the past growth, financial stability, and cyclicality of your business

3. ___ Small loans require the same detailed financial statements required for larger loans or more complex businesses

4. ___ *Pro-forma* financial statements are the historical financial statements that demonstrate how a business has performed in the past

5. ___ The Business Debt Schedule covers all current loans, leases, and other large periodic bills for which your business is responsible

6. ___ The bank will not lend to an entity that is not properly authorized to do business

C. FILL IN THE BLANK

1. While the Income Statement and _____ are typical requests, the bank may also request or require _____.

2. The _____ provides a snapshot into the past growth, financial stability, and cyclicality of your business.

3. Projected Financial Statements are normally referred to as _____ financial statements.

4. In some cases, the financials of a rapidly-growing company will demonstrate a shortage of _____ because cash generated might be needed to fund _____.

5. As part of the underwriting process, the ability of a borrower to repay all current and future _____ will be thoroughly analyzed.

6. The bank usually requests business tax returns for the last _____ years.

SHORT ANSWER

1. In Ch. 7, you learned that the bank will require you to submit several business-specific documents in addition to the required personal documents discussed in Ch. 6. Why do you think the bank requires separate personal and business-specific documents? Discuss your reasoning.

_____

_____

_____

_____

2. Imagine that you are preparing your loan application when you realize that it shows a shortage of available/free cash-flow to service the loan. In your own words, briefly explain what this means.

_____

_____

_____

_____

3. The bank doesn't always require a business to submit a business plan with the other corporate documents, but a well-crafted business plan may significantly improve your chances of being approved. In the next chapter, you will begin preparing a very basic business plan. In the space below, write a brief summary that describes your business or future business.

_____

_____

_____

_____

DISCUSSION TOPICS FOR ENTREPRENEURS

- Structure your meetings: following a specific routine for scheduled meetings, such as structuring the discussion in a Q&A format, can improve the meeting's efficiency and can help you manage the information more effectively (pg. 96). Do you have a preferred method for keeping your meetings efficient? What have you found to be most effective?

- Remember to maintain balance: Don't forget to take the time to relax and focus on other aspects of your life when given the opportunity. Entrepreneurs all too often burn out because they neglect balance and forget about the other important areas of their lives (pg. 105). What is your favorite non-business-related activity? How does this help you relax?

A. VOCABULARY MATCH

Match the term to the correct definition   *Answers*

1. Underwriting   1. ____
2. Loan Loss Rate   2. ____
3. Real Property   3. ____
4. Source of Repayment   4. ____
5. Unsecured Loans   5. ____
6. Collateral   6. ____
7. Blanket Lien   7. ____
8. Assignment of Claims   8. ____
9. Income Statement   9. ____
10. Balance Sheet   10. ____
11. Cash-Flow Statement   11. ____
12. Fixed / Term Loan   12. ____
13. Revolving Line of Credit   13. ____
14. Amortization Period   14. ____

A. A contractual agreement between you and the bank in which funds are deposited into a company-owned account that the bank can directly access as collateral

B. Any asset that a borrower pledges to a lender in order to secure approval of a loan

C. Provides data regarding cash inflows a company receives or pays from its operations, investing activities, and financing sources during a given measurement period

D. Loans that do not require specific collateral to support the loan; tend to be very costly because money is borrowed purely on your personal creditworthiness

E. A document that provides a snapshot of the financial health of a company; it highlights the assets, liabilities, and equity of the business

F. A security interest placed by a bank on some or all of a company's assets

G. The percentage of loans that do not get repaid to the bank

H. The process by which banks analyze, evaluate and document a loan prior to lending the funds.

I. Funds the bank expects (under normal circumstances) will be used to repay the loan, most often in the form of the cash-flow generated by the business

J. Also known as a revolver, it is a line of credit set at an agreed upon limit which the business can draw from when funds are needed, up to the pre-approved limit

K. A financial statement that measures a company's financial performance (sales, cost of sales, expenses, and any profit loss) during a specific measurement period

L. A loan from a bank for a specific amount that has a specified repayment schedule

M. Actual land and any structure built upon it

N. The time over which you are required to repay the loan

1. __ All banks follow an underwriting process to evaluate a prospective borrower and the risk of loaning them money

2. __ Banks strive to achieve a loan loss rate of less than 2%

3. __ Real Property is anything you personally own

4. __ The '5 C's of Underwriting' are *capacity, capital, conditions, collateral,* and *collaboration*

5. __ When underwriting a loan, the bank's first step is determining sources of repayment

6. __ The bank will analyze both the company and the industry in which it operates

7. __ Sources of repayment and collateral are the same thing

8. __ Most banks require only one source of repayment

9. __ The three most important financial statements the bank uses are the income statement, the balance sheet, and the cash-flow statement

10. __ The two primary types of small business loans are a term loan and a revolving line of credit

11. __ A term loan lets you borrow funds, pay them back, then borrow them again

12. __ The amortization period is the time over which you repay the loan

13. __ Most banks request similar items when it comes to personal documentation, although they may use bank-specific forms

14. __ Some of the data requested in the loan application packet will be requested in multiple places and on several forms

15. __ Historical / Current Financial Statements provide a snapshot into the past growth, financial stability, and cyclicality of your business

16. __ Small loans always require the same detailed financial statements required for larger loans or more complex businesses

17. __ *Pro-forma* financial statements are the historical financial statements that demonstrate how a business has performed in the past

18. __ The Business Debt Schedule covers all current loans and capital leases and may also include other large periodic bills for which your business is responsible

19. __ The bank will not lend to an entity that is not properly authorized to do business

20. __ Because it is optional, a business plan will almost never influence the bank's decision regarding loan approval

1. All banks follow a(n) _____ to evaluate the risk of loaning to a borrower.
    a. Amortization Period
    b. Underwriting Process
    c. Assignment of Claims
    d. Corporate Resolution

2. Stephen Covey is quoted as saying, "Seek first to _____, then to _____."
    a. Impress; Be Rewarded
    b. Evaluate; Act
    c. Recognize; Be Recognized
    d. Understand; Be Understood

3. What are the 5 C's of Underwriting?
    a. Capacity, Capital, Conditions, Collateral, and Character
    b. Capability, Capital, Conditions, Collateral, and Charisma
    c. Capacity, Capability, Capital, Collateral, and Character
    d. Capacity, Capital, Competence, Conditions, and Charisma

4. Most loans will require multiple _____ and _____ to support the loan.
    a. Cash-Flow Statements; Income Statements
    b. Sources of Repayment; Collateral
    c. Balance Sheets; Pro-Forma Projections
    d. Evaluations; Financial Reviews

5. Banks will sometimes file a(n) _____, which requires payments be made directly to a specified account that can be taken over by the bank if necessary.
    a. Blanket Lien
    b. Request for Proposal (RFP)
    c. Assignment of Claims
    d. Amortization Period

6. The _____ is the one the bank expects will be used to repay the loan while the _____ is normally the asset or collateral that is easiest for the bank to seize and sell.
    a. Primary Source of Repayment; Secondary Source of Repayment
    b. Collateral; Real Property
    c. Sources of Repayment; Blanket Lien
    d. Real Property; Secondary Source of Repayment

7. In most cases, a bank is going to require an additional or tertiary source of repayment called a _____, which ensures that you will personally pay back the loan if necessary.
    a. Assignment of Claims
    b. Blanket Lien
    c. Corporate Resolution
    d. Personal Guarantee

8. According to the text, the three most important statements used for the financial analysis are the _____, the _____, and the _____.
   a. Sources of Repayment; Income Statement; Balance Sheet
   b. Income Statement; Balance Sheet; Pro-Forma Projections
   c. Income Statement; Balance Sheet; Cash-Flow Statement
   d. Income Statement; Cash-Flow Statement; Pro-Forma Projections

9. The _____ is a US government agency that provides assistance and guidance to small businesses, such as help navigating the loan process.
   a. Small Business Administration (SBA)
   b. Small Business Investment Company (SBIC)
   c. Federal Deposit Insurance Corporation (FDIC)
   d. Small Loan Action Committee - Key Extra Resource (SLACKER)

10. There are two primary types of loans for small businesses: _____ and _____.
   a. SBA Express Loan; Bank Loan
   b. Term Loan; Revolving Line of Credit
   c. Term Loan; Hard Money Loan
   d. Revolving Line of Credit; Express Loan

11. A _____ lets you borrow funds, pay them back, and then borrow them again.
   a. Assignment of Claims
   b. Term Loan
   c. SBA Express Loan
   d. Revolving Line of Credit

12. In most cases, small business term loans have a(n) _____ somewhere between two and five years.
   a. Amortization Period
   b. Repayment Timeline
   c. Revolver
   d. Fixed / Term Loan

13. A _____ is generally fixed, meaning that the interest rate can be set at a fixed rate for a certain period of time.
   a. Hard Money Loan
   b. Term Loan
   c. SBA Express Loan
   d. Revolving Line of Credit

14. While the Income Statement and Balance Sheet are typical requests in the Historical/Current Financial Statements (FSs), the bank may also request or require _____.
   a. Personal Tax Returns
   b. Pro-Forma Projections
   c. Cash-Flow Statements
   d. A, B, and C

15. The _____ provide a snapshot into the past growth, financial stability, and cyclicality of your business.
    a. Business Debt Schedule
    b. Pro-Forma Financial Statements
    c. Historical Financial Statements
    d. Number of Employees Currently On Staff

16. Projected Financial Statements are normally referred to as _____.
    a. Business Debt Schedules
    b. Pro-Forma Financial Statements
    c. Historical/Current Financial Statements
    d. Corporate Tax Returns

17. The Business Debt Schedule analyzes the ability of a borrower to repay all current and future _____.
    a. Liabilities
    b. Medical Benefits
    c. Delinquent Monies
    d. Corporate Taxes

18. The bank usually requests business tax returns for the last _____ of operation.
    a. 1 Year
    b. 2-3 Years
    c. 3-5 Years
    d. 10 Years

UNIT REVIEW TEST #2 ANSWER FORM

A. VOCABULARY MATCH

1. _____
2. _____
3. _____
4. _____
5. _____
6. _____
7. _____

8. _____
9. _____
10. _____
11. _____
12. _____
13. _____
14. _____

B. TRUE OR FALSE

1. _____
2. _____
3. _____
4. _____
5. _____
6. _____
7. _____
8. _____
9. _____
10. _____

11. _____
12. _____
13. _____
14. _____
15. _____
16. _____
17. _____
18. _____
19. _____
20. _____

C. MULTIPLE CHOICE

1. _____
2. _____
3. _____
4. _____
5. _____
6. _____
7. _____
8. _____
9. _____

10. _____
11. _____
12. _____
13. _____
14. _____
15. _____
16. _____
17. _____
18. _____

UNIT #3

CH. 8 – CH. 11

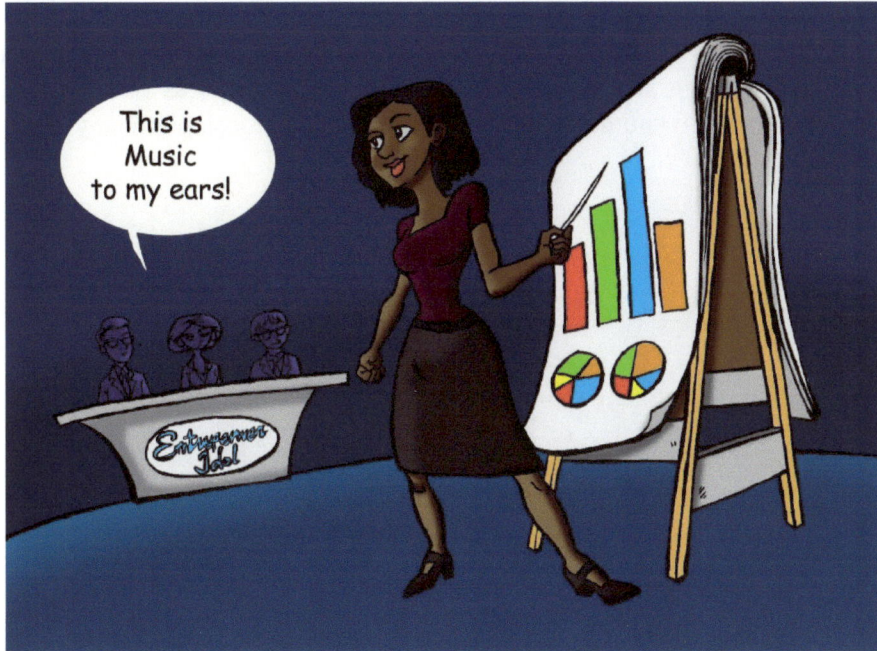

Ch. 8: Building a Credible Business Plan
Why You Need a Business Plan | The Primary Components of a Business Plan | Tailoring Your Business Plan

Ch. 9: Bank Covenants – The Mystery Explained
Understanding Loan Covenants | Types of Covenants | Important Considerations

Ch. 10: Personal Guarantees
Understanding the Guarantee | Implications & Potential Issues to Consider | Removing the Personal Guarantee

Ch. 11: Maximizing Your Chances of Loan Approval
Loan Application Checklist | Helpful Hints & Strategies

CHAPTER 8: BUILDING A CREDIBLE BUSINESS PLAN

INTRODUCTION

In Chapter 8, you familiarized yourself with one of the most important documents for entrepreneurs – the business plan. While not always required when applying for a loan, a well-crafted business plan can demonstrate credibility to a bank or other financial partners. More importantly, the process of creating a business plan is a valuable exercise in better understanding your business and goals. Think about each section of a typical business plan and consider how a bank uses the information. You should also begin outlining a business plan for your business if you have not already.

LEARNING OBJECTIVES

After reading chapter 8 and completing the review exercises in this unit of the study guide, you will be able to:

- Identify and summarize the general requirements and primary components that are included in a typical business plan

- Analyze and explain why a business plan is important, even if it is not required for the loan application

- Identify some of the characteristics of a well-crafted business plan

- Critically analyze why each section of the business plan is included, particularly in relation to the loan application process and the bank's expectations

- Create a rough draft business plan that includes all the typical components as well as any optional sections or appendices

BUSINESS PLAN COMPONENTS - PART 1

A business plan is an essential roadmap for business success and projects 3-5 years ahead, outlining the route a company intends to take to grow revenues and profits.

ELEMENTS OF A COMPLETE BUSINESS PLAN

EXECUTIVE SUMMARY

Snapshot Of Your Business – Summarizes Your Company's Profile And Goals.

- Mission statement
- Company information
- Growth highlights
- Your products/services
- Financial information
- Summarize future plans

COMPANY DESCRIPTION

Provides Information On What You Do, What Differentiates Your Business From Others, And The Markets Your Business Serves.

- Describe your target market
- Describe the nature of your business and marketplace needs that you are trying to satisfy
- Explain how your products and services meet these needs
- List the specific consumers, organizations or businesses that your company serves or will serve
- Explain the competitive advantages that you believe will make your business a success

MARKET ANALYSIS

Provides Research On Your Business Industry, Market And Competitors.

- Industry description and outlook
- Information about your target market
  - o Distinguishing characteristics
  - o Size and segmentation
  - o How much market share you expect to gain
- Competitive analysis
  - o Strengths and weaknesses of competitors
  - o Your company's competitive advantages

ORGANIZATION AND MANAGEMENT TEAM

Who Does What In Your Business? What Is Their Background And Why Are You Including Them In The Business As Board Members Or Employees?

- Organizational structure or organizational chart
- Profiles of your management team
- Ownership Information
- Board of directors' qualifications

BUSINESS PLAN COMPONENTS – PART 2

A business plan is an essential roadmap for business success and projects 3-5 years ahead, outlining the route a company intends to take to grow revenues and profits.

ELEMENTS OF A COMPLETE BUSINESS PLAN

SERVICE OR PRODUCT LINE DESCRIPTION

What Do You Sell? How Does It Benefit Your Customers? What Is The Product Lifecycle?

• A Description of Your Product / Service
• Details About Your Product's Life Cycle
• Intellectual Property
• Research and Development (R&D) Activities

MARKETING & SALES DESCRIPTION

How Do You Plan To Market Your Business? What Is Your Sales Strategy?

• An overall marketing strategy should include four different strategies:
  o A market penetration strategy
  o A growth strategy
  o Channels of distribution strategy
  o Communication strategy
• An overall sales strategy should cover how you plan to actually sell your product and includes two primary elements:
  o How you plan to use your sales force
  o Other sales activities

FUNDING REQUEST

What Are Your Funding Needs?

• How much cash do you need?
• How will you use the cash? ("Use of Proceeds")
• Where will you get the cash? ("Sources of Proceeds")
• Type of funding requested (Debt, Equity, Other)

FINANCIAL RESULTS AND PROJECTIONS

How Has The Business Done And What Do You Expect In The Future?

• Historical results (3-5 years)
• Provide 3-5 years of projections the following financial statements:
  o Income Statement
  o Balance Sheet
  o Cash Flow Forecasts
• Include analysis of financials (trend graphs, key ratios)

APPENDICES

An Appendix Is Optional, But Is A Useful Place To Include Other Information That Will Help The Reader Understand Or Appreciate Your Business.

• Resumes of key personnel
• Product collateral or marketing materials
• List of business consultants, key advisors and/or board Members

71

A. VOCABULARY MATCH

Match the term to the correct definition

Answers

1. Go-to-Market Strategy
2. Executive Summary
3. Company Description
4. Organization and Management Team
5. Market Analysis
6. Marketing and Sales Description
7. Service or Product Line Description
8. Funding Request
9. Financial Results and Projections
10. Conclusion (Summary)
11. Appendices

1. ____
2. ____
3. ____
4. ____
5. ____
6. ____
7. ____
8. ____
9. ____
10. ____
11. ____

A. This section gives the reader more details on your industry, your target market, and the company's competitive position (strengths, weaknesses, and discriminators)
B. This section includes financial results to demonstrate how the business has done in the past and project how you expect it to perform in the future; usually includes 3-5 years of historical results and financial projections along with a financial analysis
C. Includes information about where you are located, how you are organized (e.g. LLC, Corporation, Partnership, etc.), and brief descriptions of the services you provide or the products you sell.
D. A sub-section of the Marketing & Sales Description that describes the products and services you offer
E. Includes profiles of executive team and key employees, organizational structure, ownership information, and relevant qualifications of the team
F. An optional section that includes any relevant additional information such as testimonials, team resumes, marketing materials, and key advisors or consultants
G. The plan and associated strategy that a company uses to effectively launch its product or service
H. This two-part section includes both your overall marketing strategy and your sales force strategy
I. Describes your funding needs and how you will use the cash, as well as the type of funding requested
J. The first and most important section of the business plan, it describes your business as a whole and quickly tells the reader what you do and why your business will succeed
K. Essentially a condensed version of the Executive Summary, but located at the end of your business plan, it restates simply and succinctly why your business will succeed

72

1. ___ Banks will always require a business plan as part of the loan application
2. ___ Your *Go-to-Market Strategy* will normally include sections covering your business' background, your target market, major competition, your executive team, and financial projections
3. ___ The business plan should be at least 20 pages long and can sometimes exceed 70-80 pages
4. ___ The first and most important section of the business plan is the *Executive Summary*
5. ___ Both the Executive Summary and the Company Description should include in-depth analyses with lots of supporting details
6. ___ The Market Analysis section gives the reader more details on your industry and the market in which you operate
7. ___ The Organization and Management Team section is optional and should only be included if your team comprises especially well-qualified individuals
8. ___ The Marketing and Sales Description section normally includes two separate sections
9. ___ The bank expects your business plan to include both historical and projected financial results
10. ___ You should include additional information about your business (such as testimonials, resumes, marketing materials, etc.), if available, in an optional Appendices section at the end of the business plan

C. FILL IN THE BLANK

1. A business plan can be important especially if you have a major change in your _____ that requires new analysis and projections.
2. A well-developed business plan lays out the _____ for your business.
3. The _____ is the plan a company uses to effectively sell or launch its product or service
4. The first and most important section of your business plan is the _____.
5. The executive summary and company description sections are _____ rather than _____.
6. The market analysis section gives the reader more details on your _____, the _____ in which you operate, and reasons why it is appealing.
7. After the Executive Summary, the _____ may be the most important section of your business plan.
8. An overall marketing strategy normally includes four different strategic elements: a _____ strategy (how you will establish your business), a _____ strategy (how you will continue to grow), a _____ strategy that describes how you distribute your products, and a _____ strategy that describes the key ways you communicate with your target customers.
9. Although not required, an _____ section can be included to highlight additional information that is pertinent to the business.

SHORT ANSWER

For this project, you will begin preparing a basic business plan that includes several of the most important sections in a real business plan. As you read through Ch. 8, think about what the bank looks for and what you should include in your business plan. After reading the chapter, prepare a series of bullet points and highlights that summarize the major aspects of each of the following business plan components:

A. Executive Summary (refer to the draft you made in the previous chapter exercises)
B. Company Description
C. Product & Services
D. Marketing & Sales Description

    A. Executive Summary

_____
_____
_____
_____

    B. Company Description

_____
_____
_____
_____

    C. Product & Services

_____
_____
_____
_____

    D. Marketing & Sales Description

_____
_____
_____
_____

DISCUSSION TOPIC FOR ENTREPRENEURS

- Plan out action items: action items are the next steps you must take to accomplish something. Take time to plan out your action steps whenever you complete a task or project (pg. 107). Do you have a large task ahead that would be more effectively broken down into smaller, more manageable tasks? How might you do this more effectively?

CHAPTER 9: BANK COVENANTS – THE MYSTERY EXPLAINED

As you learned in Chapter 9, loan covenants are requirements highlighting what you can and cannot do with your business if you receive a bank loan. You learned about each of the primary categories and types of covenants as well as their applications. As you prepare to complete the following exercises, think about how covenant agreements impact your business and its operations, and consider ways to avoid common mistakes that lead to covenant violations.

LEARNING OBJECTIVES

After reading chapter 9 and completing the review exercises in this unit of the study guide, you will be able to:

- Clearly define and differentiate between the two primary categories of loan covenants as well as the corresponding sub-categories within each

- Analyze and explain why loan covenants exist and why the bank uses them before approving a loan application

- Analyze how bank covenants can influence a business' decisions, capital, and overall focus

- Identify potential risks and downsides associated with loan covenants, particularly in terms of how covenants can impact a business and its operations

COVENANTS - RESTRICTIVE

PROTECTIVE
(YOU MUST)

RESTRICTIVE
(YOU CAN'T)

AFFIRMATIVE

- ↗ Operate Business Successfully
- ↗ Maintain Collateral For Loan
- ↗ Tell Bank How You Are Doing
- ↗ Provide Financial Reports
- ↗ Obey All Laws Including Paying Taxes
- ↗ Maintain Insurance Coverages
- ↗ Make Payments When Due

NEGATIVE

- ↘ Sell/Remove Collateral
- ↘ Borrow More $ Without Banks Permission
- ↘ Loan $ To Others
- ↘ Sell Business Or Buy Other Businesses
- ↘ Pay Out Too Much To Owners Or Shareholders
- ↘ Change Out Key Members Of Managers Team

*The covenants described above are typical samples, but are not exhaustive. Your covenants will vary based on your situation.

A. VOCABULARY MATCH

Match the term to the correct definition   *Answers*

1. Covenants   1. ____
2. Financial Covenants   2. ____
3. Profitability Covenants   3. ____
4. Leverage Covenants   4. ____
5. Cash Flow Covenants   5. ____
6. Restrictive Covenants   6. ____
7. Liquidity Covenants   7. ____
8. Measurement Period   8. ____

A. A covenant stipulating minimum profitability required of the borrower over a specific measurement period. This covenant may also stipulate the maximum loss or negative profitability that a borrower is allowed.
B. Instructions and details on what you can and cannot do in your business, as defined by the lender
C. The second major category of covenants, these dictate a company's specific financial requirements related to liquidity, profitability, or leverage
D. These covenants ensure the availability of liquid assets (current ratio, net working capital)
E. The first major categories of covenants, these dictate what a party can and cannot do
F. The point in time or period of time over which a company's performance is measured
G. These stipulate the minimum cash flow a borrower must generate to cover expected debt service obligations (principal and interest payments) required to be met by the borrower
H. These covenants stipulate the maximum leverage or outstanding debt that a borrower may incur based on profitability achieved over a specified measurement period

B. COVENANT EXERCISES

The following exercise will take you through some basic covenant calculations. You may recall that in Chapter 9 Jessica and Mike discussed various covenants that the bank might put in place. For the purposes of this exercise, assume that Jessica ultimately gets her loan approved and is thus accountable for all normal requirements, processes, and official documentation that usually accompany a loan approval. With that in mind, think about what you've read so far and use the enclosed Balance Sheet and Income Statement to complete Jessica's Custom Clothing, Inc., located at the end of this workbook chapter.

Using the following information, determine the values and write your answers in the yellow boxes within the table below

The bank has required the following five covenants as a condition for approving Jessica's loan:

Liquidity Covenants:
- Current Ratio must remain greater than 1.5
- Quick Ratio must remain greater than 1.0

Profitability Covenants:
- Jessica's annual net income must be $250,000 or greater
- Jessica's Quarterly Net Income must be greater than $0.

Leverage/Debt Coverage Covenant
- The company's Fixed Charge Coverage Ration (FCC) must be greater than 1.20

PART I: VALUATION AND FINANCIALS

Code	Definitions	Covenant Code Key	Jessica's Value (at 6/30/19)
CA	Current Assets	A	
CL	Current Liabilities	B	
Inventory	Inventory	C	
NI (TTM)	Net Income	D (for last year (TTM))	
NI (Q2)	Net Income	E (for latest quarter - Q2)	
EBITDA (TTM)	Earnings Before Interest, Taxes, Depreciation or Amortization	F (for last year (TTM))	
EBITDA (Q2)	Earnings Before Interest, Taxes, Depreciation or Amortization	O (for latest quarter - Q2)	
CPLTD	Current portion of LTD, including capital leases	G	
LTD	Long Term Debt, Including capital leases	H	
TD	Total Debt = All Debt Combined (CPLTD + LTD + LOC)	= G + H + P	
Lease Exp	Capital Lease Payments	I	
TA	Total Assets	J	
TL	Total Liabilities	K	
Net Worth	Net Worth = TA - TL	= J - K	
Int Exp	Interest Expense	L	
D&A	Depreciation & Amortization Expense	M	
Total Equity	Total Equity	N	
LOC	Line of Credit	P	

PART II: COVENANT COMPLIANCE

Calculate Jessica's value for each covenant and determine whether or not she is in compliance with each covenant. Write your answer in the yellow boxes in the table below.

Covenant Calculations Exercise

Liquidity (Working Capital) Covenants

Name	Measures	Calculations	Covenant Requirement	Jessica's Value	In Compliance?
Current Ratio	Businesses short-term liquidity	CA / CL	Must remain greater that 1.5		
Quick Ratio	Businesses short-term liquidity	(CA - Inventory) / CL	Must remain greater than 1.0		

Profitability Covenants

Name	Measures	Calculations	Covenant Requirement	Jessica's Value	In Compliance?
Annual Net Income	Income produced during a particular measurement period	Value taken directly from Income Statement	Annual net income must be greater than $250,000		
Quarterly Net Income	Income produced during a particular measurement period	Value taken directly from Income Statement	Quarterly net income must be greater than $0 - (No loss quarters)		

Leverage / Debt Coverage Covenants

Name	Measures	Calculations	Covenant Requirement	Jessica's Value	In Compliance?
Fixed Charge Coverage Ratio (FCC)	Ability to service debt with income generated by business	(NI+Int Exp+Lease Exp+Dep + Amort)/(Int Exp +Lease Exp + CPLTD)	Must remain greater than 1.20		

Notes:
Be sure not to double count capital lease expense in denominator of FCC calculation.
All values are calculated as of 6/30/19 using Jessica's Custom Clothing financial statements included above.

Balance Sheet

Jessica's Custom Clothing, Inc.

As of 6/30/2019

Assets		Covenant Code
Current Assets		
Cash	$75,000	
Net Accounts Receivable	$1,450,000	
Inventory	$250,000	C
Prepaid Expenses	$125,000	
Total Current Assets	$1,900,000	A
Fixed (Long-Term) Assets		
Land	$950,000	
Buildings	$1,300,000	
Property & Equipment - Net	$150,000	
Furniture & Fixtures	$75,000	
Other Assets	$35,000	
Total Net Fixed Assets	$2,510,000	
Total Assets	$4,410,000	J

Liabilities & Stockholder's Equity		Covenant Code
Current Liabilities		
Accounts Payable	$550,000	
Line of Credit	$385,000	P
Long Term Debt, Current Portion	$286,517	
Capitalized Lease Obligations, Current Portion	$75,000	I — G
Accrued Payroll & Benefits	$225,000	
Accrued Payables	$25,000	
Total Current Liabilities	$1,546,517	B
Long Term Liabilities		
Long Term Debt, Less Current Portion	$643,465	
Capitalized Lease Obligations, Less Current Portion	$120,000	H
Other Long-Term Liabilities	$75,000	
Total Long-Term Liabilities	$838,465	
Total Liabilities	$2,384,982	K
Stockholder's Equity		
Common Stock, $0.01 Par Value, 1,000,000 Shares Authorized, 500,000 Issued & Outstanding	$5,000	
Additional Paid-in Capital	$345,000	
Retained Earnings	$1,570,332	
Current Year Net Income	$104,685	
Total Shareholders Equity (Net Worth)	$2,025,017	N
Total Liabilities & Stockholder's Equity	$4,410,000	

Jessica's Custom Clothing, Inc.

TTM Income Statement - Summary By Quarter

	Quarter 3 7/1/18- 9/30/18	Quarter 4 10/1/18- 12/31/18	Quarter 1 1/1/19 - 3/31/19	Quarter 2 4/1/19 - 6/30/19	Trailing 12 Months (TTM)	Covenant Code
Revenues						
Clothing Sales (On-lIne)	$1,210,000	$1,195,000	$1,300,000	$1,200,000	$2,500,000	
Manufacturing (Private Label)	$120,000	$75,000	$120,000	$150,000	$270,000	
Design & Development	$50,000	$40,000	$50,000	$25,000	$75,000	
Total Revenue	**$1,380,000**	**$1,310,000**	**$1,470,000**	**$1,375,000**	**$5,535,000**	
Cost of Goods Sold						
Clothing Sales (On-line)	$302,500	$298,750	$325,000	$300,000	$625,000	
Manufacturing (Private Label)	$30,000	$18,750	$30,000	$37,500	$67,500	
Design & Development	$10,000	$8,000	$10,000	$5,000	$15,000	
Total Cost of Goods Sold	**$342,500**	**$325,500**	**$365,000**	**$342,500**	**$1,375,500**	
Gross Profit	**$1,037,500**	**$984,500**	**$1,105,000**	**$1,032,500**	**$4,159,500**	
Employee Pay	$320,000	$320,000	$320,000	$325,000	$1,285,000	
Overtime Pay				$40,000	$40,000	
Owner Bonuses	$0	$25,000	$45,000	$115,000	$185,000	
Accounting	$10,000	$10,000	$10,000	$10,000	$40,000	
Sales & Marketing	$170,000	$170,000	$170,000	$170,000	$680,000	
Depreciation & Amortization	$25,000	$25,000	$25,000	$25,000	$100,000	
401(k) Contributions	$25,000	$25,000	$25,000	$25,000	$100,000	
Employee Incentives	$50,000	$50,000	$50,000	$50,000	$200,000	
Insurances	$40,000	$40,000	$40,000	$40,000	$160,000	
Internet Services	$5,000	$5,000	$5,000	$5,000	$20,000	
Lease Payments	$15,000	$15,000	$15,000	$15,000	$60,000	
Legal Fees	$7,500	$7,500	$7,500	$7,500	$30,000	
Meals Business	$2,500	$2,500	$2,500	$2,500	$10,000	
Miscellaneous	$10,000	$10,000	$10,000	$10,000	$40,000	
Consultants	$70,000	$70,000	$70,000	$70,000	$280,000	
Term Loan Pmts - Interest	$12,347	$11,581	$10,815	$10,049	$44,793	
Software	$5,000	$5,000	$5,000	$5,000	$20,000	
Taxes, Payroll	$55,500	$55,500	$55,500	$72,750	$239,250	
Telephone	$2,500	$2,500	$2,500	$2,500	$10,000	
Travel	$25,000	$25,000	$25,000	$25,000	$100,000	
Utilities	$15,000	$15,000	$15,000	$15,000	$60,000	
Total Operating Expenses	**$865,347**	**$889,581**	**$908,815**	**$1,040,299**	**$3,704,043**	
Profit Before Taxes (PBT)	**$172,153**	**$94,919**	**$196,185**	**-$7,799**	**$455,457**	
					8.2%	
Interest Expense	*$12,347*	*$11,581*	*$10,815*	*$10,049*	*$44,793*	L
Earnings Before Interest & Taxes (EBIT)	**$184,500**	**$106,500**	**$207,000**	**$2,250**	**$500,250**	
EBIT Margin	13.4%	8.1%	14.1%	0.2%	**9.0%**	
Taxes 40%	$73,800	$42,600	$82,800	$900	$200,100	
Net Income	**$98,353**	**$52,319**	**$113,385**	**-$8,699**	**255,357**	D
				E		
EBITDA Calculation						
EBIT	$184,500	$106,500	$207,000	$2,250	$500,250	
Depreciation & Amortization	*$25,000*	*$25,000*	*$25,000*	*$25,000*	*$100,000*	M
EBITDA	**$209,500**	**$131,500**	**$232,000**	**$27,250**	**$600,250**	F
Note: Minor errors in values due to rounding				O		

82

CHAPTER 10: PERSONAL GUARANTEES

INTRODUCTION

We've all heard horror stories in which a business fails and the bank takes everything – even the kitchen sink. These are usually examples of what happens when the bank has taken all other measures and then must enforce the personal guarantee. As you learned in Chapter 10, personal guarantees are pledges by a business and its owner that a loan will be repaid in full. This is an extremely important topic because the personal guarantee is usually directly linked to your own personal finances (in addition to your business' finances) and almost all loans will require a business owner to sign a personal guarantee. As you complete the following exercises, think about the ways in which you can evaluate a guarantee's requirements and potential risks.

LEARNING OBJECTIVES

After reading chapter 10 and completing the review exercises in this unit of the study guide, you will be able to:

- Explain what a guarantee is and why the bank requires borrowers to sign multiple guarantees

- Differentiate between personal guarantees and business guarantees

- Explain the bank's rationale for requiring multiple guarantees

- Describe the ways in which a business can have the personal guarantee removed

- Assess the reasons that a business might choose to shift banks

A. VOCABULARY MATCH

Match the term to the correct definition   *Answers*

1. Commercial Guarantee   1. ____
2. Business Guarantee   2. ____
3. Personal Guarantee   3. ____
4. Due Diligence   4. ____

A. A pledge made by the business itself (the legal entity) that guarantees repayment of a loan. It typically includes company assets used to collateralize the loan

B. A legal document executed by the company that guarantees to the bank that they will be repaid. It generally includes both a business guarantee and a personal guarantee

C. The investigation a banking team conducts to review and underwrite a loan. It also refers to the reviews that a company might do when it selects one lender over another

D. A pledge made by the owner of a business that guarantees repayment of a loan. It is used to collateralize the loan, and often includes a pledge of the personal assets of the individual, making the guarantee for repayment in the event the business fails to repay its debt obligations

B. TRUE OR FALSE

1. ____ The Commercial (or Corporate) Guarantee is both a Business Guarantee and a Personal Guarantee

2. ____ A Personal Guarantee is usually mandatory until a business has been operating and growing profitably for some time

3. ____ A Personal Guarantee assures that the loan will be repaid, even by the owner's non-business assets if necessary

4. ____ The Personal Guarantee is permanent and cannot be modified or removed

5. ____ It is always easier for a banker to be flexible and 're-underwrite' an existing customer's loan than it is to underwrite a completely new loan for a new customer

6. ____ As long as your business is bankable, there is no risk in shifting your bank relationship

C. FILL IN THE BLANK

1. A _____ is both a business guarantee and a personal guarantee.

2. Personal guarantees require _____ consent in many states.

3. _____ is the investigation or review of individual assets before taking any certain action.

4. The _____ and its associated _____ serve as a backup source of repayment, especially for small businesses and first-time borrowers.

5. If your business has problems and is unable to pay back a loan, the bank may enforce the _____ and seek repayment from both you and any of your major shareholders who were also required to sign the personal guarantee.

6. Although there are some exceptions, most personal guarantees are _____ in nature, meaning that a large portion of your net worth might be at risk even if it exceeds the amount you borrowed due to accrued penalties and interest.

7. As your business grows and becomes profitable enough to stand on its own financially, it's best to limit the _____ you personally have tied to the business.

8. Although removing a personal guarantee can be difficult, highly _____ businesses should have no problem asking for its removal.

CORE CONCEPT REVIEW

KEY THEMES & CONCEPTS:

- What is a guarantee and how does it affect both your business and your personal finances?
- Why does the bank require a potential loan recipient to sign a guarantee?
- What steps can be taken to remove the personal guarantee?
- What are some of the reasons, benefits, and disadvantages to shifting banks?

SHORT ANSWER

1. How is a personal guarantee different than a covenant? Compare and contrast the two terms and provide at least one example that demonstrates the differences.

_____

_____

_____

_____

2. According to the text, the bank often requires a personal guarantee in addition to the corporate guarantee until a business has maintained profitable operations for an extended period. Why do you think the bank requires both guarantees? What must you do to get the personal guarantee removed?

_____

_____

_____

_____

A few years ago, Dominic applied for a small bank loan to help him launch and grow a small hip-hop label based in San Diego. After months of hard work, dedication, and consistency, Dominic was able to demonstrate the long-term viability of his record label to the bank and he received a revolving line of credit to help him finance the growth of his business. In the two years that have followed, Dominic's record label has steadily grown, adding new artists and releasing several acclaimed hip-hop records that garnered national attention. All the while, Dominic has never failed to meet a payment on time and he has openly communicated with the bank anytime a potential challenge has arisen. At this point, he wants to limit any significant financial liabilities tied to the business and he believes he might have enough leverage to have the personal guarantee removed from his loan package.

Given this information, would you describe Dominic's business as bankable? Why or why not? Think about what you learned in Chapter 10 and try to identify the various factors that might prove beneficial in demonstrating Dominic's creditworthiness. How has Dominic met the general requirements usually necessary to have the personal guarantee removed? Are there any elements of Dominic's business that might prevent him from having the personal guarantee removed? Finally, what else could Dominic do to further improve his bankability and demonstrate to the bank that he is creditworthy enough to have the personal guarantee removed?

DISCUSSION TOPIC FOR ENTREPRENEURS

- Weigh your options: before making a decision, always consider the alternatives and any potential consequences that might result. Think about the opportunity cost, in terms of the time and money that could be spent elsewhere (pg. 143). Describe a situation where you have multiple possible courses of action. Describe how much each path will "cost" in terms of time and money. Which one will produce the greatest "return on investment (ROI)"?

CHAPTER 11: MAXIMIZING YOUR CHANCES OF LOAN APPROVAL

INTRODUCTION

At this point, you are fast approaching the final stages of the loan application process. As you come closer to finalizing your loan application, you will need to ensure that each and every required document is present and completed. Use the checklist in Chapter 11 to help you verify that each item is finished and ready for submission. Try to identify any documents that must be completed and, if possible, review them with your advisor or instructor for more clarification.

LEARNING OBJECTIVES

After reading chapter 11 and completing the review exercises in this unit of the study guide, you will be able to:

- Review the requirements for submitting a loan request package
- Prepare and organize all the required materials for submission
- Use the 'Bank Loan Approval Checklist' to verify that you have compiled all required materials and completed all required sections

BANK LOAN APPROVAL CHECKLIST

☑ **Determine Your Funding Needs**
• Analyze the uses of your loan proceeds to calculate size of loan required

☑ **Check Your Personal Credit Report & Your Business Dun & Bradstreet (D&B) Report**
• Correct any mistakes
• Be able to explain any unusual information

☑ **Prepare Your Business Plan**
• Make sure your business plan is thorough and concise
• (See chapter on Building A Credible Business Plan for more details)

☑ **Collect Historical Financial Statements**
• Have the last 2-3 years of Income Statements ready

☑ **Prepare 3-5 Years Of Financial Projections (Pro-Forma Financial Projections)**
• Income Statement, Balance Sheet & Cash Flow statements

☑ **Collect Current Financial Statements and Reports**
• Current Income Statement, Balance Sheet & Cash Flow statements
• Accounts Receivable & Accounts Payable Aging

☑ **Complete Your Personal Financial Statement**
• Collect all bank statements, investment statements & documentation of all sources of income

☑ **Determine Which Type Of Loan Or Line Of Credit You Need**
• Explore various options available from your bank & the Small Business Administration (SBA)

☑ **Prepare Your Personal Resume And "Business" Resume, If Appropriate**
• Include information concerning your business successes & why you will be a good credit risk

☑ **Collect Your Income Tax Returns For Submission.**
• A minimum of two years is generally required

☑ **Understand Your Sources Of Repayment**
• Understand primary, secondary & other sources of loan repayment

☑ **Understand & Document Your Sources Of Collateral**
• Prepare a list of all your significant assets as well as documentation regarding market value

☑ **Collect All Your Company's Legal Documents**
• These will vary depending on what type of legal entity your business is (Corporation, LLC, Partnership or Sole Proprietorship)
• These include formation documents (Articles or Certificate of Incorporation), Bylaws, business licenses & Certificates of Good Standing (GSC)
• Operating or Partnership Agreements for LLC's or Partnerships

☑ **Learn Who Is On Your Banking Team**
• Introduce yourself to key banking team members if possible

☑ **Prepare For "Interview Questions" - Convince The Bank You Are Credit -Worthy**
• Be ready to explain why you need the funds; how you will use them & how you intend to pay them back
• Be prepared to address any key issues or concerns

☑ **Understand Your Loan Covenants**
• Review these with your banker

☑ **Review All Loan Documents Carefully & Submit For Approval**
• Review these with your banker

☑ **Celebrate Your Loan Approval!**
• Keep all original loan documents in a safe place

A. FILL IN THE BLANK

1. _____ are documents that describe the past performance, profitability, and recurring expenses of a business, while _____ are related financial estimates and expectations based on this expected future performance.

2. The bank will most likely require _____ years of financial projections as part of your loan application.

3. In order to fill out your _____ you will need your bank statements, payroll records and information about your investments.

4. Although these vary depending on the type of business, a company's _____ include Articles of Incorporation, bylaws, and Certificates of _____.

5. The bank will evaluate your sources of _____ and sources of _____ when they underwrite your loan.

DISCUSSION TOPICS FOR ENTREPRENEURS

- In many cases, a bank will not lend you as much money as you want or need. Just like the bank evaluates your sources of repayment, as an entrepreneur you should always have alternative sources of funding just in case your loan doesn't get approved or is approved but for an amount less than you need or desire. What other sources of funding might be available to you? Which ones would be the easiest to obtain?

- No one will understand your business as much or as well as you do. Try not to get frustrated when someone else fails to see the value that you see in the business or cannot understand its potential for future success. What are some ways that you can document or demonstrate the current and future potential and value of your business?

A. VOCABULARY MATCH

Match the term to the correct definition   _Answers_
1. Go-to-Market Strategy   1. ____
2. Executive Summary   2. ____
3. Organization and Management Team   3. ____
4. Market Analysis   4. ____
5. Service or Product Line Description   5. ____
6. Funding Request   6. ____
7. Financial Results and Projections   7. ____
8. Covenants   8. ____
9. Profitability Covenants   9. ____
10. Leverage Covenants   10. ____
11. Cash-Flow Covenants   11. ____
12. Liquidity   12. ____
13. Measurement Period   13. ____
14. Personal Guarantee   14. ____
15. Due Diligence   15. ____

A. A pledge made by the owner of a business that guarantees repayment of a loan. It is used to collateralize the loan and often includes a pledge of the personal assets of the individual, making the guarantee for repayment in the event the business fails to repay its debt obligations

B. These covenants stipulate the maximum leverage or outstanding debt that a borrower may incur based on profitability achieved over a specified measurement period; used to ensure that you are not taking on too much debt

C. A sub-section of the Marketing & Sales Description that describes your products and services

D. The financials that demonstrate how the business has done in the past, and project how you expect it to perform in the future; usually includes 3-5 years of historical results and financial projections along with a financial analysis

E. The point in time or period of time over which a company's performance is measured

F. The first and most important section of the business plan; it describes your business as a whole and quickly tells the reader what you do and explains why you believe your business will succeed

G. Describes your funding needs and how you will use the cash, as well as the type of funding requested

H. This section of the business plan gives the reader more details on your industry, your target market, and the company's competitive position (strengths, weaknesses, and discriminators)

I. A covenant stipulating minimum profitability required of the borrower over a specific measurement period. This type of covenant may also stipulate the maximum loss or negative profitability that a borrower is allowed. It is often associated with corresponding leverage covenants and/or cash flow covenants

J. This section of the business plan includes profiles of executive team and key employees, organizational structure, ownership information, and relevant qualifications of the team

K. A measure of a company's liquid, or readily available, assets

L. Instructions and details on what you can and cannot do in your business, as defined by the lender

M. The strategy and associated plan a company uses to effectively launch or sell its product or service

N. The investigation a banking team conducts to review and underwrite a loan. It also refers to the reviews that a company might do when it selects one lender over another

O. These covenants stipulate the minimum cash flow a borrower must generate to cover expected debt service obligations (principal and interest payments) required to be met by the borrower

B. TRUE OR FALSE

1. ___ Banks will always require a business plan as part of the loan application
2. ___ The business plan should be at least 30 pages long
3. ___ The first and most important section of the business plan is the *Executive Summary*
4. ___ The Executive Summary and the Company Description should include very detailed analyses
5. ___ The Organization and Management Team section is optional and should only be included if your team comprises especially well-qualified individuals
6. ___ The bank expects your business plan to include both historical and projected financial results
7. ___ If possible, you should include additional positive information about your business (such as testimonials, resumes, marketing materials, etc.) in an optional Appendices section at the end of the business plan
8. ___ Covenants are standardized and regulated so you can never request modifications or negotiate with the lender on which covenants to include
9. ___ Restrictive Covenants are those that tell you what you cannot do with your business
10. ___ Protective Covenants establish repayment schedules that guarantee to the bank that they will be repaid in full
11. ___ Financial Covenants are those that require a company to meet certain financial goals generally related to liquidity, cash-flow, or leverage
12. ___ Profitability Covenants ensure that you are not taking on too much debt
13. ___ The *Commercial (or Corporate) Guarantee* is both a Business Guarantee and a Personal Guarantee
14. ___ A Personal Guarantee assures that the loan will be repaid, even by the owner's non-business assets if necessary
15. ___ The Personal Guarantee is permanent and can never be modified or removed

1. A new or modified business plan can be important if you have a major change in your _____ that requires new analysis and projections.
   a. Funding
   b. Business Strategy
   c. Pro-Forma Projections
   d. Any of the above

2. The _____ is the strategy and associated plan a company uses to effectively launch or sell its product or service.
   a. Business Plan
   b. Funding Request
   c. Market Analysis
   d. Go-to-Market Strategy

3. The first and most important section of your business plan is the _____.
   a. Executive Summary
   b. Company Description
   c. Marketing & Sales Description
   d. Funding Request

4. The market analysis section gives the reader more details on your _____, the _____ in which you operate, and reasons why it is appealing.
   a. Industry; Market
   b. Business; Industry
   c. Distinguishing Characteristics; Industry
   d. Strengths & Weaknesses; Market

5. According to the text, the _____ is the second most important section of your business plan after the Executive Summary.
   a. Company Description
   b. Market Analysis
   c. Marketing & Sales Description
   d. Organization & Management Team

6. Although not required, a(n) _____ section can be included to highlight additional information that is pertinent to the business, such as testimonials and marketing materials.
   a. Conclusion
   b. Branding & Reputation
   c. Appendices
   d. Glossary

7. _____ give you instructions and details on what you can and cannot do with your business while you owe money to the bank.
   a. Sources of Repayment
   b. Covenants
   c. Expectations
   d. Corporate Resolutions

8. The two major categories of covenants are _____ and _____ covenants.
   a. Restrictive; Financial
   b. Preventive; Fiscal
   c. Good; Bad
   d. Preemptive; Defensive

9. Restrictive covenants come in two primary forms: _____ and _____ covenants.
   a. Restrictive; Financial
   b. Affirmative; Negative
   c. Positive; Negative
   d. Preemptive; Defensive

10. _____ covenants identify what a company must do while _____ covenants identify what it cannot do.
    a. Restrictive; Financial
    b. Affirmative; Negative
    c. Positive; Negative
    d. Fun; Boring

11. Financial covenants lay out specific financial requirements related to _____, _____, and _____.
    a. Revenue; Expenses; Debt
    b. Equity; Debt; Profitability
    c. Liquidity; Profitability; Leverage
    d. Cash-Flow; Valuation; Profitability

12. _____ is a measure of the readily-available assets of a company
    a. Liquidity
    b. Cash-Flow
    c. Valuation
    d. Profitability

13. Covenants help keep a business focused on items like _____ and _____, areas where a lender sees the most risk.
    a. Cash-Flow; Profitability
    b. Debt; Leverage
    c. Growth; Staffing
    d. Benefits; Employee Turnover

14. A _____ is both a business guarantee and a personal guarantee.
    a. Financial Covenant
    b. Corporate / Commercial Guarantee
    c. Business Plan
    d. Loan Application

15. _____ is the investigation or review of individual assets before taking any certain action.
    a. A Credit Report
    b. The Measurement Period
    c. The Go-to-Market Strategy
    d. Due Diligence

16. The _____ and its associated _____ serve as a backup source of repayment, especially for small businesses and first-time borrowers.
    a. Personal Guarantee; Commercial Guarantee
    b. Corporate Guarantee; Commercial Guarantee
    c. Financial Guarantee; Personal Guarantee
    d. Go-to-Market Strategy; Commercial Guarantee

17. If your business has problems and is unable to pay back a loan, the bank may enforce the _____ and seek repayment from both you and any major shareholders who were required to sign it as well.
    a. Personal Guarantee
    b. Commercial Guarantee
    c. Financial Covenants
    d. Sources of Repayment

18. Although there are some exceptions, most personal guarantees are _____ in nature, meaning that a large portion of your net worth might be at risk even if it exceeds the amount you borrowed.
    a. Restricted
    b. Unlimited
    c. Finite
    d. Predetermined

19. As your business grows and becomes profitable enough to stand on its own financially, it's best to limit the _____ you personally have tied to the business.
    a. Income
    b. Liabilities
    c. Sources of Repayment
    d. Personal Guarantee

20. Although removing a personal guarantee can be difficult, highly _____ businesses should have no problem asking for its removal or reduction.
    a. Leveraged
    b. Productive
    c. Bankable
    d. Established

UNIT REVIEW TEST #3: ANSWER FORM

A. VOCABULARY MATCH

1. ____
2. ____
3. ____
4. ____
5. ____
6. ____
7. ____
8. ____

9. ____
10. ____
11. ____
12. ____
13. ____
14. ____
15. ____

B. TRUE OR FALSE

1. ____
2. ____
3. ____
4. ____
5. ____
6. ____
7. ____
8. ____

9. ____
10. ____
11. ____
12. ____
13. ____
14. ____
15. ____

C. MULTIPLE CHOICE

1. ____
2. ____
3. ____
4. ____
5. ____
6. ____
7. ____
8. ____
9. ____
10. ____

11. ____
12. ____
13. ____
14. ____
15. ____
16. ____
17. ____
18. ____
19. ____
20. ____

UNIT #4

CH. 12 – CH. 16

Ch. 12: Signing the Loan Documents

Preparing the Loan Execution Documents | Evaluating the Bank's Rationale | Helpful Hints

Ch. 13: Successfully Building Your Banking Relationship

The Primary Goals of the Banking Relationship | What Not to Do | Going Above & Beyond

Ch. 14: Help! I've Violated a Bank Covenant

Preparing an Action Plan | Meeting with the Bank | Strategies for Avoiding Violations

Ch. 15: Success! Loans Approved

Looking Back | Looking Ahead

Ch. 16: Selecting Your Source of Capital – Alternatives to Bank Debt

Options & Alternatives to Bank Debt | Evaluating Ownership & Equity | Advantages & Disadvantages

Chapter 12: Signing the Loan Documents

Congratulations, you are nearly finished with the loan application process! It is important that you understand that, up until now, you have not actually entered into any legally-binding agreement with the bank. Chapter 12 discussed the process of signing the loan documents along with explanations for each document to be signed. As you prepare to complete the following exercises, think about the bank's rationale for requesting each document. Also take note of any particular requirements or clauses that might have unexpected consequences.

Learning Objectives

After reading chapter 12 and completing the review exercises in this unit of the study guide, you will be able to:

- Prepare yourself for signing the bank loan documents
- Describe each of the required loan documents and the requirements laid out within each
- Explain the bank's rationale for requesting each document
- Differentiate between various loan documents and the specific intent of each document

LOAN EXECUTION DOCUMENTS

DOCUMENT	WHAT?	WHY?	HELPFUL HINTS
PROMISSORY NOTE	This is the actual loan document that lays out the details of your loan. It covers your covenants, rights, and obligations related to the loan.	The promissory note documents all the loan provisions.	Read it carefully to understand all the loan provisions. Check all the numbers carefully to make sure the loan amount and repayment schedule are correct. Pay close attention to the covenants listed in the "Default" section. Make sure you understand all of those. If you have any questions, be sure to ask your attorney or CPA.
CORPORATE RESOLUTION – AUTHORITY TO BORROW	This is the official legal document that gives the company's official authorization and approval for your business to legally enter into the binding contracts associated with the loan, which include all the documents listed here.	The bank needs to ensure that the loan is properly authorized by the company and that you (or whoever signs the documents) have the corporate authority to obligate the company to borrow the funds and repay the loan.	Make sure that this document is reviewed by your attorney and entered into the corporate minute book or company records.
COMMERCIAL GUARANTEE (Generally Incorporates an Individual Personal Guarantee)	This document provides the bank with the businesses guarantee (& that of major shareholders) that the loan will get repaid.	It provides the bank with a backup source of repayment. The signers will be required to make personal assets available if the bank has been unable to collect the debt from the business.	This document removes virtually any right to avoid being personally responsible for the debt that the business owes to the bank. Pay close attention to the amount of the guarantee, generally unlimited, even if the loan amount is set.
COMMERCIAL SECURITY AGREEMENT	This document grants a security interest in (& claim to) all collateral provided to support the loan. It also lists covenants related to the listed collateral.	The document provides the bank with a source of repayment should the borrower default. It describes all the collateral that the bank is claiming as part of its security.	The bank will expect all listed collateral to be free from other liens. Make sure you haven't pledged any of the items to other creditors or investors. Understand the restrictions on what you can and can't do to/with the collateral.
TRUST AGREEMENT	This document ensures that any borrower's Trust authorizes the execution of the loan documents. It is required when the borrower has a trust that may have a claim to the collateral that the borrower is pledging for the loan.	This ensures the bank will have access to the collateral in event of loan default, otherwise the Trust might protect the assets of the borrower from a claim by the bank.	Contact your attorney to make sure the trust authorizes you to execute. The trust might need to be amended to allow the trustee(s) to execute documents that pledge collateral.
AGREEMENT TO PROVIDE INSURANCE	This document ensures that you maintain sufficient insurance to protect the bank's collateral	This provides the bank with assurance that their loan will be secured properly, even in the event of a casualty that damages or destroys some of the collateral you provided.	Make sure that the type and amount of insurance coverage is reasonably available and affordable for your business. Occasionally, this holds up a loan because the business is under-insured or lacks a certain type of insurance required by the bank.

A. VOCABULARY MATCH

Match the term to the correct definition

Answers

1. Small Business Lending Group (SBLG)
2. Loan Execution Documents
3. Promissory Note / Loan Agreement
4. Corporate Resolution
5. Commercial Guarantee
6. Commercial Security Agreement
7. Security Interest
8. Trust Agreement
9. Trust
10. Agreement to Provide Insurance

1. ____
2. ____
3. ____
4. ____
5. ____
6. ____
7. ____
8. ____
9. ____
10. ____

A. A relationship where property is held by one party (the trustee) for the benefit of another person or persons (the beneficiaries)
B. The official document that gives the company's official authorization and approval to legally enter into the binding contracts associated with the loan
C. Grants a security interest in and claim to all collateral provided to support the loan; also lists covenants related to the listed collateral
D. Makes sure that you will adequately insure the assets you pledge to the bank.
E. The full or partial ownership of, or lien on, an asset assigned to a bank as collateral for a loan
F. A subset of the bank's commercial lending organization that usually handles clients with annual revenues less than $5 million (although this amount varies by bank)
G. Provides the bank with the business' guarantee that the loan will be repaid
H. Ensures that any borrower's trust authorizes the execution of the loan documents. It is required when the borrower has a trust that may have a claim to the collateral being pledged for the loan
I. This is the actual loan document that describes all the loan provisions. It lays out the details of your loan and covers the covenants, rights, and obligations of the loan
J. The collective documents required by the bank to finalize the loan application process.

B. TRUE OR FALSE

1. ___ The Promissory Note normally documents all loan provisions and lays out the details of the loan, such as covenants, rights, and obligations
2. ___ The Commercial Guarantee is the legal document that gives official authorization and approval for you and your business to legally enter into a binding contract
3. ___ The bank's claim to all collateral you provide to support the loan is an example of a *Security Interest*
4. ___ The Trust Agreement functions as a contractual handshake between a borrower and lender to demonstrate their mutual trust that each will fulfill the agreed upon requirements

5. ___   Many entrepreneurs fail to fully understand the extent of their commitments and restrictions until after signing the loan documents

C. FILL IN THE BLANK

1. The _____ is a subset of the bank's commercial lending organization and usually handles clients with annual revenues between $1 million and $5 million.
2. The document that gives official authorization and approval for you and your business to legally enter into a binding loan contract is called the _____.
3. The _____ provides the bank with a backup source of repayment in the event that the business has problems meeting its financial obligations.
4. The Commercial Security Agreement grants a _____ to all collateral you provide to the lender to support the loan.
5. A _____ is a relationship in which property is held by one party (the _____) for the benefit of another person or persons (the _____).

CORE CONCEPT REVIEW

SHORT ANSWER

1. Explain the differences between the following loan items. How are they similar and how are they different? Specifically, identify the primary focus of each document and why the bank requires it.
   a. Corporate Resolution
   b. Commercial Guarantee
   c. Commercial Security Agreement

_____
_____
_____
_____

DISCUSSION TOPIC FOR ENTREPRENEURS

- Express gratitude: always take time to thank anyone that has helped you along the way. A small gesture of appreciation, such as a handwritten note, gift card, or nice bottle of wine, can make a significant impact and help to strengthen long-term networking opportunities (pg. 156). What are some other ways that you can thank the people who have helped you?

CHAPTER 13: SUCCESSFULLY BUILDING YOUR BANKING RELATIONSHIP

As you have learned by now, your relationship with a bank and its banking team plays an important role in successfully obtaining a bank loan. In Chapter 13, we further explored the role of your banking relationship and what you can do to demonstrate reliability and build credibility with the bank. You learned that a beneficial partnership requires the right balance between communication, character, and confidence. Think about the various strategies you have learned for demonstrating credibility and developing a professional yet personable relationship with the banking team. As you begin the following exercises, you should consider what the bank wants to see from a borrower – and, more importantly, what they do not want to see.

LEARNING OBJECTIVES

After reading chapter 13 and completing the review exercises in this unit of the study guide, you will be able to:

- Identify effective strategies and practices for strengthening your banking relationship
- Determine your primary goals when it comes to building your banking relationship
- Explain the ways that credibility, character, and communication can influence your relationship with the bank
- Describe how bankability and leverage can influence your ability to borrow or shift banks

A. VOCABULARY MATCH

Match the term to the correct definition   *Answers*

1. Contingencies   1. ____
2. Credit Rating Agencies   2. ____
3. Dun & Bradstreet   3. ____
4. "Becoming the Hunted"   4. ____

A. The point at which a successful company, having maintained a proven track record of growth and profitability, becomes highly desirable to virtually every bank
B. Conditions that must be met before the bank will give final approval for a loan
C. This credit rating agency is the world's leading source of commercial and financial information on businesses
D. Institutions that measure your financial strength using data that you and other businesses provide

B. TRUE OR FALSE

1. ____ *Contingencies* are conditions that must be met before the bank will give final approval on a loan

2. ____ One of the best ways to establish yourself as a good customer is to maintain a solid record of paying back the principal plus interest payments on time

3. ____ Getting the bank to like you should be one of your four primary goals for building a banking relationship

4. ____ Although you should regularly communicate with the banking team, you should never attempt to make friends and get to know the team on a more personal level

5. ____ Building credibility with the bank is mostly symbolic and has little impact on long-term financial benefits or opportunities

6. ____ One of the best ways to build credibility is to notify the bank every time your business encounters a financial obstacle, no matter how insignificant

7. ____ Compared to less established businesses, highly bankable businesses with a proven track record of growth and profitability have significantly more influence and leverage when seeking bank financing

C. FILL IN THE BLANK

1. _____ are conditions that must be met before the bank will give final approval for a loan.

2. The bank can be one of your most important financial partners because it has the capacity to fund almost your entire _____.

3. _____ like Dun & Bradstreet (D&B) measure your financial strength using data that you and other businesses provide.

4. You should _____ with the bank frequently enough that they know how you and your business are doing.

5. _____ are a key factor in business success and your banking relationship is no different.

6. Building _____ with the bank allows for more borrowing in the future.

7. Your goal is to build a relationship in which the bank _____ you, _____ you, and has faith that you _____ and what drives its success.

8. At some point in the life of a successful company, a business becomes _____ to virtually _____.

9. A proven track record of _____ and _____, especially during tough times, makes it much easier to find banks that want to loan you money.

10. As you grow larger and more profitable, you will have more _____ to improve your terms with the bank.

CORE CONCEPT REVIEW

SHORT ANSWER

1. As you read the chapter, pay attention to what Jessica did during the loan submission process. Why do you think her loan was approved without contingencies? What did she do that helped set her apart from other applicants?

   _____
   _____
   _____
   _____

2. Review the four primary goals listed on pg. 162 under 'Building Your Banking Relationship.' Think about why each individual goal influences the overall application, and then provide at least one reason for why each goal is important.

   _____
   _____
   _____
   _____

3. Recall the example of Sam and his client, Mr. Smith. Identify at least two things that Mr. Smith did to strengthen his relationship with the bank. How did his actions influence his loan decision?

_____
_____
_____
_____

4. Why do you think character and communication are so important? How do these impact the bank's decisions in the short-term and long-term?

_____
_____
_____
_____

5. "Just because you can shift banks doesn't mean you should" (pg. 171). Consider this statement and think about the pros & cons of shifting banks. Next, come up with two reasons you might stay with a bank and two reasons you might consider shifting.

_____
_____
_____
_____

DISCUSSION TOPICS FOR ENTREPRENEURS

- Disengage every once in a while: vacations exist for a reason. If you've been working tirelessly for months on end, reward yourself with a brief vacation or other break from work when you have the opportunity. It's important to periodically 'recharge your batteries' (pg. 160). When was the last time you "disengaged"? How did it help your productivity when you returned to work/school?

- First impressions matter: you never get a second chance to make a great first impression. Make sure you make an impact by preparing ahead of time and knowing your audience (pg. 160). Can you think of a time when you made a terrible first impression? What could you have done differently?

- Get to know your team: one of the best ways to strengthen a professional relationship is by connecting with them on a personal level. A friendly phone call or light-hearted conversation can help you get to know them better and make them more compelled to go out of their way to help you (pg. 165). Can you think of other ways to positively build your team?

Chapter 14: Help! I've Violated a Bank Covenant

Introduction

We first discussed bank covenants and the ways that they influence your loan package and business operations in Chapter 9. However, at some point you may find yourself faced with an accidental covenant violation. In Chapter 14, you learned how to address and resolve minor covenant violations. Recall that, although minor violations can be recoverable, the bank takes covenant violations very seriously nonetheless. As you prepare to complete the following exercises, imagine that you have violated a covenant and think about how you will proactively address violations quickly, effectively, and in a way that doesn't damage your credibility.

Learning Objectives

After reading chapter 14 and completing the review exercises in this unit of the study guide, you will be able to:

- Identify and explain what actions must be taken in the event of a covenant violation
- Assess a covenant violation and prepare a corrective action plan to effectively address the covenant violation
- Describe various ways in which the bank can react to a covenant violation
- Identify and assess various ways in which a business can unknowingly violate a bank covenant
- Prepare for various scenarios in which a covenant violation negatively affects the recipient's bank loan

Chapter 14 Exercises

A. Vocabulary Match

Match the term to the correct definition

1. Corrective Action Plan
2. Acceleration Clause
3. Forbearance

Answers
1. ____
2. ____
3. ____

A. A special agreement between the lender and the borrower to delay a bank's default provisions for customers experiencing short-term financial difficulty
B. A provision in the loan documents that allows a lender to require a borrower to repay all or part of an outstanding loan if certain requirements are not met
C. A plan for overcoming or addressing a covenant violation with the bank

B. True or False

1. ___ If you accidentally violate a covenant, you should notify the bank right away before attempting to assess and resolve the situation

2. ___ The first thing you should do after violating a covenant is fully analyze the situation to determine what went wrong

3. ___ A Proactive Action Plan lays out your strategy for overcoming or addressing a covenant violation

4. ___ The Acceleration Clause permits the bank to require all future loan payments due and payable immediately

5. ___ The bank is usually held responsible for ensuring that loan covenants accurately and realistically reflect a company's assets and expenses

C. Fill in the Blank

1. While all covenants are important and require your full compliance, in most cases, _____ can be recoverable.

2. The first thing you should do in the event of a covenant violation is _____ the situation to determine exactly what happened, the _____ of the violation, and why it happened.

3. After violating a covenant, you should prepare a _____ to help you proactively address the situation with the bank.

4. Remember that the bank wants to lend you money and has an _____ to help you, but only if they are convinced that you are a good _____.

5. Even if the bank makes an error, it is always the company's _____ to understand what their loan requirements are and to make sure they are all met.

6. A bank will sometimes issue a _____ which allows it to delay loan provisions while a borrower is experiencing _____ financial difficulty.

SHORT ANSWER

1. Imagine that you accidentally violated a covenant and must now explain yourself to the bank. Review the four steps on pages 175 and 176. Provide a short response for each of the four steps. Pay close attention to what you must cover during each step. What will you say and how will you demonstrate that you understand what went wrong?

    _____

    _____

    _____

    _____

DISCUSSION TOPIC FOR ENTREPRENEURS

- Don't ever burn bridges: never damage your professional network by acting unprofessionally or reacting badly toward someone else. You never know when you might need to rely on that person for assistance (pg. 179). Can you think of two or three ways to stay connected to your network? Which one is easiest for you to maintain?

Chapter 15: Success! Loans Approved!

Introduction

Congratulations! You now have the tools and knowledge that will help you successfully apply for and receive a bank loan. The journey can be a long and difficult one, with complications and even the occasional sleepless night. That said, entrepreneurs are a resilient and dedicated group. If you can persevere and maintain a consistent forward momentum, you will no doubt find yourself successful in the end.

Learning Objectives

After reading chapter 15 and completing the review exercises in this unit of the study guide, you will be able to:

- Identify various ways in which a potential borrower can maximize their chances of loan approval
- Identify some of the primary characteristics of a winning loan application
- Describe what the bank looks for in a loan application package

Chapter 15 Exercises

Core Concept Review

Short Answer

1. Think about the principles and strategies that you have learned over the course of the book. Identify at least two skills, strategies, or concepts that were particularly useful for you. What impact did they have on you and why? How can you use these newly acquired skills to further develop your business?

   _____

   _____

   _____

   _____

2. At this point, you are much more familiar with the general loan application process and its associated requirements. Now think about the challenges and potential complications you will have to overcome in the future. What parts of the loan application process might present the most challenges for you? How can you prepare to address and overcome these obstacles?

   _____

   _____

   _____

   _____

3. What was the most valuable lesson you learned from the book? What made it valuable to you?

   _____

   _____

   _____

   _____

4. Character and integrity are hugely important during the application process, but they can be just as important after your loan gets approved. Small gestures can have a significant impact on long-term relationships and should never be ignored. What are some ways that you can express your gratitude to your advisors and banking team for helping you during this process?

   _____

   _____

   _____

   _____

CHAPTER 16: SELECTING YOUR SOURCE OF CAPITAL
ALTERNATIVES TO BANK DEBT

INTRODUCTION

In this supplemental chapter, we discussed several alternative sources of financing and debt available to most entrepreneurs. As we discussed, bank loans can be difficult to obtain for less-established businesses and startups. For this reason, many entrepreneurs will want to consider alternative sources of financing to grow their business in its early stages. In Chapter 16, we explored various debt and financing options as well as their advantages and disadvantages. To help you prepare for the chapter exercises, think about which of these debt sources you might consider using for your business. Compare and contrast their unique characteristics, strengths, and weaknesses. Likewise, pay close attention to the discussion on debt versus equity and consider whether or not full ownership and control are a high priority. You may find that some of the alternative sources of financing seem to be a better fit than a traditional bank loan.

LEARNING OBJECTIVES

After reading chapter 16 and completing the review exercises in this unit of the study guide, you will be able to:

- Identify, define, and describe some of the primary alternative sources of funding available to small businesses
- Compare and contrast these debt alternatives with traditional bank loans
- Evaluate their own personal resources and determine which, if any, can be used as potential sources of funding
- Evaluate the potential risks associated with non-bank debt and other alternative sources of funding (such as unsecured loans through friends and family)
- Compare and contrast debt versus equity, particularly in terms of how maintaining ownership and control differs from selling equity in exchange for capital.
- Evaluate & assess the various options available and identify at least two alternative sources of debt that might be appropriate for their own business

A. VOCABULARY MATCH

Match the term to the correct definition   *Answers*

1. Capital   1. ____
2. Sources of Capital   2. ____
3. Bootstrapping   3. ____
4. Liquid Assets   4. ____
5. Opportunity Cost   5. ____
6. Promissory Note   6. ____
7. Peer to Peer (P2P) Lending   7. ____
8. Seed Funding   8. ____
9. Factoring   9. ____
10. Subordinated Debt (Mezzanine   10. ____

Funding)   11. ____

11. Hard Money Loans   12. ____
12. Equity   13. ____
13. OPM   14. ____
14. Crowdfunding

A. Using your personal resources (such as savings) to finance your company; it is generally the cheapest and easiest source of capital
B. In terms of financial decisions, this is the value or income that could have been gained by investing available funds elsewhere
C. Debt taken on by a company that is subordinated in repayment priority to senior debt owed to a bank or other lending institution
D. Refers to the cash available to fund a company's operations
E. The first external funding a startup business raises, it is generally provided by friends and family or angel investors
F. A financing process in which a business sells some or all of its accounts receivable to a factoring company, thus giving the factoring company the right to collect the payment. The business sells the receivable at a discount to its value in exchange for immediate payment to the business
G. Assets that can be converted to cash quickly; these generally include cash, marketable securities, and collectible accounts receivable
H. A written agreement between parties in which one party promises to repay funds to the other
I. A stock or any other security representing an ownership interest
J. An increasingly popular source of financing in which companies use an online portal to describe their product and solicit investors for the project, often before it is widely available
K. A specific type of asset-based loan financing in which a borrower receives funds (normally secured by real property) - generally at very high interest rates
L. The practice of lending money to unrelated individuals without going through a traditional financial intermediary such as a bank or other traditional financial institution
M. Refers to the various financing options available to most businesses, each of which has distinct advantages and disadvantages
N. Short for 'other people's money,' allows you to share some of the risk with investors who put up capital in the form of cash used to purchase equity or debt in the company

B. True or False

1. ___ *Bootstrapping* refers to using your own existing resources to fund the initial growth of your business
2. ___ Personal sources of capital include liquid assets, cash value life insurance, 401K loans, and friends & family
3. ___ One of the most frequently used sources of capital is debt financing or loans from friends and family
4. ___ Loans that involve friends or family are known as personal (unsecured) loans
5. ___ Factoring allows you to sell a large percentage of your accounts receivable in exchange for cash, thereby giving the buyer right to collect payment
6. ___ Exchanging equity for cash allows you to retain complete ownership and control of your business
7. ___ Risk-sharing in the form of using outside capital investment is referred to as 'getting down with OPP'
8. ___ Seed funding uses an online portal in which you describe your product/service and solicit investors in exchange for pre-sale access or equity shares

C. Fill in the Blank

1. Using your existing personal resources as an initial source of capital is commonly referred to as _____.
2. Savings, brokerage accounts, certificates of deposit, and cash available from insurance all fall into the same category, _____.
3. Items categorized under cash on hand or readily available are sometimes referred to as _____.
4. You should always keep an _____ available, as it would be unwise to use every source available to you.
5. Outside of using your own cash on hand, the source of capital most frequently used to fund a business is _____.
6. While Friends & Family loans are normally unsecured, another (more expensive) option is _____ loans from _____.
7. _____ through online platforms (sometimes called _____) is a new source of funding in which individuals can borrow from a variety of different lenders.
8. _____ are another frequently-used method of startup funding, and some people have built up significant _____ over time prior to launching their business.
9. When a business needs to borrow more than a bank is willing to lend, one option is using _____ debt.
10. If you are not going to borrow money, one other primary source of funding involves selling _____ in your business in exchange for _____.
11. If you sell equity in your business, you will no longer have full _____ and _____ of the company.
12. Investors who purchase equity in your business are usually most concerned with the _____ of your business.

13. Another reason many businesses choose equity over debt is the issue of _____ and _____.

14. _____ uses an online portal in which you describe your product/service and solicit investors in exchange for pre-sale access or equity shares.

CORE CONCEPT REVIEW

1. In the last chapter, you learned that there are many financing options available other than bank debt. After reading Chapter 16, think about your own funding needs and then pick at least two different alternative sources of funding that might be viable options for you. What about these sources might make them more viable than other sources of funding?

   _____

   _____

   _____

   _____

2. As you now know, *bootstrapping* refers to funding your startup using your own personal cash and available resources. Examine your available personal resources and describe which of these could be used to bootstrap your business. Do you have any other resources available that can be used?

   _____

   _____

   _____

   _____

3. Whether or not they realize it, most beginning entrepreneurs consider the opportunity cost of one financial decision versus another. In your own words, explain the concept of opportunity cost as it relates to you and your financial choices. Then provide at least one example that relates to opportunity cost.

   _____

   _____

   _____

   _____

DISCUSSION TOPIC FOR ENTREPRENEURS

- Brainstorm with other people: Take advantage of group discussions and don't hesitate to discuss new ideas with your network. Other people can offer valuable perspectives and feedback that you might not have considered on your own (pg. 186). Can you think of a time when you and a group you were involved with used brainstorming techniques to develop a creative solution? Why was this successful?

   _____

UNIT REVIEW TEST #4: CH. 12 – 16

A. VOCABULARY MATCH

Match the definitions

	Answers
1. Small Business Lending Group (SBLG)	1. ____
2. Promissory Note	2. ____
3. Corporate Resolution (Authority to Borrow)	3. ____
4. Commercial Guarantee	4. ____
5. Commercial Security Agreement	5. ____
6. Security Interest	6. ____
7. Trust Agreement	7. ____
8. Trust	8. ____
9. Agreement to Provide Insurance	9. ____
10. Acceleration Clause	10. ____
11. Forbearance Agreement	11. ____
12. Capital	12. ____
13. Sources of Capital	13. ____
14. Bootstrapping	14. ____
15. Liquid Assets	15. ____
16. Opportunity Cost	16. ____
17. Peer to Peer (P2P) Lending	17. ____
18. Seed Funding	18. ____
19. Factoring	19. ____
20. Subordinated Debt (Mezzanine Funding)	20. ____
21. Hard Money Loans	21. ____
22. Equity	22. ____
23. OPM	23. ____
24. Crowdfunding	24. ____

A. Using your personal resources (such as savings) to finance your company; generally the cheapest and easiest source of capital

B. In terms of financial decisions, this is the value or income you could have made by investing available funds elsewhere

C. Provides the bank with the business' guarantee that the loan will be repaid

D. A relationship where property is held by one party (the trustee) for the benefit of another person or persons (the beneficiaries)

E. Short for 'Other People's Money,' allows you to share some of the risk with investors who put up capital in the form of cash used to purchase equity in the company

F. Refers to a company's financial assets (such as cash), as well as any factories, machinery, or other equipment owned by the company

G. Assets that can be converted to cash quickly; generally includes cash, marketable securities, and collectible accounts receivable

H. The practice of lending money to unrelated individuals, or "peers", without going through a traditional financial intermediary such as a bank or other traditional financial institution

I. The actual loan document that describes all the loan provisions. It lays out the details of your loan and covers the covenants, rights, and obligations of the loan

J. Grants a security interest in and claim to all collateral provided to support the loan; also lists covenants related to the listed collateral

K. The full or partial ownership of or lien on an asset assigned to a bank as collateral for a loan

L. A subset of the bank's commercial lending organization that usually handles clients with annual revenues less than $5 million

M. Ensures you will adequately insure the assets you pledge to the bank. The promissory note generally includes covenants related to sufficient insurance coverage and outlines the types and amounts required

N. Ensures that any borrower's trust authorizes the execution of the loan documents. It is required when the borrower has a trust that may have a claim to the collateral being pledged for the loan

O. A provision in the loan documents that allows a lender to require a borrower to repay all or part of an outstanding loan if certain requirements are not met

P. An increasingly popular source of financing in which companies use an online portal to describe their product and solicit investors for the project, often before it is widely available

Q. The official legal document that gives the company's official authorization and approval to legally enter into the binding contracts associated with the loan

R. A financing process in which a business sells some or all of its accounts receivable to a factoring company, thus giving the factoring company the right to collect the payment. The business sells the receivable at a discount to its value in exchange for immediate payment to the business

S. A special agreement between the lender and the borrower to delay a banks default provisions for customers experiencing short-term financial difficulty

T. Debt taken on by a company that is subordinated in repayment priority to senior debt owed to a bank or other lending institution

U. Refers to the various financing sources available to most businesses, each of which has distinct advantages and disadvantages

V. The first external funding a startup business raises, it is generally provided by friends and family or angel investors

W. A specific type of asset-based loan financing in which a borrower receives funds secured by real property, usually at a very high interest rate

X. A stock or any other security representing an ownership interest

B. TRUE OR FALSE

1. ___ The Small Business Lending Group (SBLG) is a subset of a bank's lending organization that usually handles clients within a certain annual revenue range (usually $1 to $5 million)

2. ___ The bank's claim to all collateral you provide to support the loan is an example of a *Security Interest*

3. ___ The Trust Agreement functions as a contractual handshake between a borrower and lender to demonstrate their mutual trust that each will fulfill the agreed upon requirements

4. ___ Many entrepreneurs fail to fully understand the extent of their commitments and restrictions until after signing the loan documents

5. ___ *Contingencies* are conditions that must be met before the bank will give final approval on a loan

6. ___ One of the best ways to establish yourself as a good customer is to maintain a solid record of paying back the principal plus interest payments on time

7. ___ Although you should regularly communicate with the banking team, you should never attempt to make friends and get to know the team on a more personal level

8. ___ Building credibility with the bank is mostly symbolic and has little impact on long-term financial benefits or opportunities

9. ___ One of the best ways to build credibility is to notify the bank every time your business encounters a financial obstacle, no matter how insignificant

10. ___ Compared to less established businesses, highly bankable businesses with a proven track record of growth and profitability have significantly more influence and leverage when seeking bank financing

11. ___ If you accidentally violate a covenant, you should first notify the bank right away before attempting to assess and resolve the situation

12. ___ A Proactive Action Plan lays out your strategy for overcoming or addressing a covenant violation

13. ___ The Acceleration Clause permits the bank to require all future loan payments due and payable immediately

14. ___ The bank is usually held responsible for ensuring that loan covenants accurately and realistically reflect a company's assets and expenses

15. ___ *Bootstrapping* refers to using your own existing resources to fund the initial growth of your business

16. ___ Personal sources of capital include liquid assets, cash value life insurance, 401K loans, and brokerage accounts

17. ___ The most frequently used source of capital is loans / equity from friends and family

18. ___ Factoring allows you to sell a large percentage of your accounts receivable to a company in exchange for cash, thereby giving them right to collect payment

19. ___ Exchanging equity for capital allows you to retain complete ownership and control of your business

20. ___ Subordinated Debt uses an online portal in which you describe your product/service and solicit investors in exchange for pre-sale access or equity shares

1. The _____ is a subset of the bank's commercial lending organization and usually handles clients with annual revenues between $1 million and $5 million.
   a. SBIC
   b. SBLG
   c. SBA
   d. D&B

2. The _____ is the actual loan document that you sign to execute a loan; it covers the covenants, rights, and obligations of the loan.
   a. Promissory Note
   b. Executive Summary
   c. Business Plan
   d. Security Agreement

3. The legal document that gives official authorization and approval for you and your business to legally enter into a binding loan contract is called the _____.
   a. Commercial Security Agreement
   b. Personal Guarantee
   c. Commercial Guarantee
   d. Corporate Resolution

4. The _____ provides the bank with a backup source of repayment in the event that the business has problems meeting its financial obligations.
   a. Commercial Guarantee
   b. Personal Guarantee
   c. Commercial Security Agreement
   d. Corporate Resolution

5. The Commercial Security Agreement grants a(n) _____ to all collateral you provide to the lender to support the loan.
   a. Trust
   b. Security Interest
   c. Assignment of Claims
   d. Amortization Schedule

6. A(n) _____ is a relationship in which property is held by one party for the benefit of another person or persons.
   a. Trust
   b. Security Interest
   c. Commercial Security Agreement
   d. Commercial Guarantee

7. _____ are conditions that must be met before the bank will give final approval for a loan.
    a. Exceptions
    b. Contingencies
    c. Covenants
    d. Bribes

8. Credit rating agencies like _____ measure your financial strength using data that you and other businesses provide.
    a. The SBA
    b. Abercrombie & Fitch
    c. Stratton Oakmont
    d. Dun & Bradstreet

9. When you make a financial decision, the _____ is the benefit, value, or income you could have made by investing available funds elsewhere
    a. Equity
    b. Economic Value Added
    c. Opportunity Cost
    d. Production Possibility Frontier

10. Building _____ with the bank allows for more borrowing in the future.
    a. Credibility
    b. Sand Castles
    c. Leverage
    d. Equity

11. _____ refers to using your own existing resources to fund the initial growth of your business.
    a. Seed Funding
    b. Factoring
    c. Bootstrapping
    d. Leverage

12. A proven track record of _____ and _____, especially during tough times, makes it much easier to find banks that want to loan you money.
    a. Communication; Openness
    b. Growth; Profitability
    c. Productivity; Success
    d. Ownership; Control

13. While all covenants are important and require your full compliance, in most cases, _____ can be recoverable.
    a. Minor Violations
    b. Significant Violations
    c. Violations Involving Fraud
    d. Defaulting on the Loan

14. The first thing you should do in the event of a covenant violation is _____ to determine exactly what happened and to what extent.
    a. Fully Analyze the situation
    b. Notify the Bank
    c. Review your balance sheets and expense reports
    d. Ask the Bank what happened

15. After violating a covenant, you should prepare a _____ to help you proactively address the situation with the bank.
    a. Go-to-Market Strategy
    b. Corrective Action Plan
    c. Remedial Steps Assessment
    d. Short and witty anecdote

16. Remember that the bank wants to lend you money and has a(n) _____ to help you, but only if they are convinced that you are a good _____.
    a. Incentive; Credit Risk
    b. Motive; Investment
    c. Objective; Liability
    d. Purpose; Borrower

17. Even if the bank makes an error, it is always the company's _____ to understand what their loan requirements are and to make sure they are all met.
    a. Prerogative
    b. Right
    c. Responsibility
    d. Objective

18. A bank will sometimes issue a(n) _____ which allows it to delay certain loan provisions while a borrower is experiencing short-term financial difficulty.
    a. Security Interest
    b. Forbearance Agreement
    c. Acceleration Clause
    d. Pro-Forma

UNIT REVIEW TEST #4: ANSWER FORM

A. VOCABULARY MATCH

1. ____
2. ____
3. ____
4. ____
5. ____
6. ____
7. ____
8. ____
9. ____
10. ____
11. ____
12. ____

13. ____
14. ____
15. ____
16. ____
17. ____
18. ____
19. ____
20. ____
21. ____
22. ____
23. ____
24. ____

B. TRUE OR FALSE

1. ____
2. ____
3. ____
4. ____
5. ____
6. ____
7. ____
8. ____
9. ____
10. ____

11. ____
12. ____
13. ____
14. ____
15. ____
16. ____
17. ____
18. ____
19. ____
20. ____

C. MULTIPLE CHOICE

1. _____
2. _____
3. _____
4. _____
5. _____
6. _____
7. _____
8. _____
9. _____

10. _____
11. _____
12. _____
13. _____
14. _____
15. _____
16. _____
17. _____
18. _____

NOTES

132

CONCLUSION

Looking back on your journey & looking ahead toward your future plans

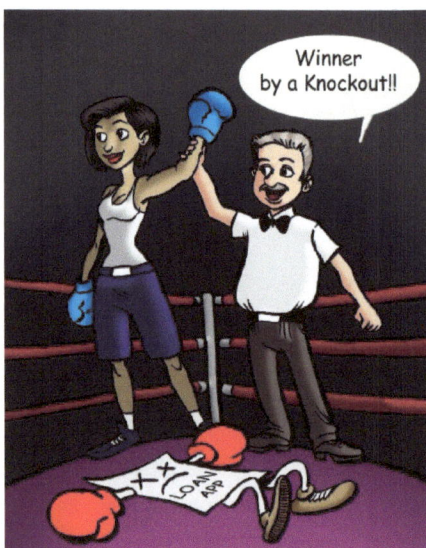

AN ENTREPRENEUR'S WORK DAY NEVER ENDS

Congratulations! You've reached the end of the *Approved! Workbook & Study Guide*. Give yourself a high five and a strong pat on the back, you deserve it! Just think – only a short time ago, you might have considered yourself completely unprepared to undergo the bank loan application process. By now, you probably feel like an entrepreneur extraordinaire. But your job isn't done! In fact, it's just beginning.

You are now prepared to enter the real-life world of business and entrepreneurship. The road ahead will be long and difficult at times, but as an entrepreneur, you are more than capable of persevering and adapting to meet each challenge as you confront it. In fact, it is this very process that enables entrepreneurs, executives, and startup owners alike to develop their skills, knowledge, and experience. Failure can be good! And, believe me, you will fail at times – probably more than once. But at least now you will have the skills and insight to know how to thrive in the face of such opposition. The majority of businesses fail within only a few years but yours doesn't have to be one of them.

We hope that you have enjoyed your time working through the *Approved! Workbook & Study Guide*. It is our greatest hope that you found value in the exercises and approaches presented within. Please do not hesitate to reach out with any comments, concerns, suggestions, or questions you might have. We look forward to hearing from you.

SEND US YOUR FEEDBACK

We would love to hear from you! *Approved!* would not exist if it weren't for entrepreneurs like you, and as such, we are here to listen to what you have to say! Whether you're a student, instructor, first-time entrepreneur, or seasoned business owner, everyone is encouraged to reach out to us – We look forward to hearing all your questions, comments, suggestions, and humorous anecdotes and we'll do our best to respond. Your feedback is the key to making *Approved!* the best resource available.

VISIT US ONLINE

Funding Success is dedicated to working directly with entrepreneurs, business owners, and other professionals to help them grow their business through interactive, immersive programs and resources based in real-world principles and expert insight.

If you enjoyed the *Approved! Workbook & Study Guide*, be sure to check out the other resources available on www.FundingSuccess.com. Download digital PDF and eBook files to keep *Approved!* with you on the go, and check out our online community forum where entrepreneurs and industry leaders can interact and exchange ideas, questions, and contact information for networking and business exchanges.

GLOSSARY OF TERMINOLOGY

Amortization Period: The time over which you are required to repay the loan

Ancillary Services: Additional services offered by the bank and usually related to financial assistance and wealth management

Assets: Items (tangible and intangible) owned by a person or company, and regarded as having value. Used as collateral for loans and obligations to a bank.

Assignment of Claims: A contractual agreement between you and the bank in which funds are typically deposited into a company-owned account that the bank can directly access as collateral

Balance Sheet Ratios: Financial ratios calculated by using financial data from balance sheets

Balance Sheet: A document that provides a snapshot of the financial health of a company; it highlights the assets, liabilities, and equity of the business

"Bankability": Refers to a business that is financially stable with adequate sources of repayment and sufficient prospects for future success

Banks:

- **Local / Community Banks:** The smallest category of bank in terms of assets under management and number of branch locations
- **Regional / Multi-Regional Banks:** Along with local community banks, this category is smaller and tends to be more accommodating and flexible compared to a large bank
- **Multinational Banks:** The largest category of bank, these banks tend to offer more ancillary services and branch locations
- **Credit Unions:** Unlike traditional banks, these are actually member-owned non-profit organizations and subject to membership requirements

Banking Team:

- **Relationship Banker:** Manages the relationship with the business owner and sources loans to decide with his/her team if a loan is viable
- **Supervising Banker:** Oversees all loans produced by Relationship Bankers
- **Credit Analyst / Credit Committee:** Analyzes the company, executive team, and industry as well as sources of repayment and collateral
- **Credit Officer:** Responsible for reviewing and deciding whether or not to approve a loan
- **Group Manager / Regional Vice President:** Responsible for the operations of one or more regional offices and reviews loan packages with Credit Officer (or Credit Committee)

Blanket Lien: A security interest placed by a bank on some or all of a company's assets

Bootstrapping: Using your personal resources (such as savings) to finance your company; generally the cheapest and easiest source of capital

Business Plan: A well-developed business plan lays out your 'roadmap to success.' It should include key information that helps the reader understand all the critical aspects of your business. A typical business plan will include several different sections, each of which focuses on a specific aspect of the business.

- **Executive Summary:** The first and most important section of the business plan, it describes your business as a whole and quickly tells the reader what you do and why your business will succeed

- **Company Description:** This section of the business plan includes information about where you are located, how you are organized (e.g. LLC, Corporation, Partnership, etc.), and brief descriptions of the services you provide or the products you sell

- **Organization and Management Team:** This section of the business plan includes profiles of executive team and key employees, organizational structure, ownership information, and relevant qualifications of the team

- **Market Analysis:** This section gives the reader more details on your industry, your target market, and the company's competitive position (strengths, weaknesses, and discriminators)

- **Marketing and Sales Description:** This two-part section includes both your overall marketing strategy and your sales force strategy

- **Service or Product Line Description:** A sub-section of the Marketing & Sales Description that describes the products and services you offer

- **Funding Request:** Describes your funding needs and how you will use the cash, as well as the type of funding requested

- **Financial Results and Projections:** The financials demonstrate how the business has done in the past and project how you expect it to perform in the future; usually includes 3-5 years of historical results and financial projections along with a financial analysis

- **Conclusion (Summary):** Essentially a condensed version of the Executive Summary, it restates simply and succinctly why your business will succeed

- **Appendices:** An optional business plan section that includes any relevant additional information such as testimonials, team resumes, marketing materials, and key advisors or consultants

Capital: Refers to a company's financial assets (such as cash), as well as any factories, machinery, or other equipment owned by the company

Cash-Flow Statement: Provides data regarding cash inflows a company receives or pays from its operations, investing activities, and financing sources during a given measurement period

Collateral: The assets a borrower pledges to a lender to secure approval of a loan. Usually includes things that the business owns, such as real estate, equipment, inventory, and the accounts receivable

Covenants: Instructions and details on what you can and cannot do in your business. Covenants come in several categories and forms.

- **Restrictive Covenants**: One of the two major categories of covenants, these dictate what a party can and cannot do; usually divided into two categories

- **Affirmative Covenants**: Also known as a *protective covenant*, it identifies what a company must do

- **Negative Covenants**: Also known as a *restrictive covenant*, it identifies what a company must not do

- **Financial Covenants**: The second major category of covenants, these dictate a company's specific financial requirements related to liquidity, profitability, or leverage
- **Profitability Covenants**: A covenant stipulating minimum profitability required of the borrower over a specific measurement period. This covenant may also stipulate the maximum loss or negative profitability, that a borrower is allowed. This covenant is often associated with corresponding leverage covenants and/or cash flow covenants
- **Leverage Covenants**: These covenants stipulate the maximum leverage or outstanding debt that a borrower may incur based on profitability achieved over a specified measurement period; used to ensure that you are not taking on too much debt
- **Cash-Flow Covenants**: These covenants stipulate the minimum cash flow a borrower must generate to cover expected debt service obligations (principal and interest payments) required to be met by the borrower
- **Liquidity Covenants**: This type of covenant ensures the availability of liquid assets (current ratio, net working capital)

Crowdfunding: An increasingly popular source of financing in which companies use an online portal to describe their product and solicit investors for the project, often before it is widely available

Due Diligence: The investigation a banking team conducts to review and underwrite a loan. It also refers to the reviews that a company might do when it selects one lender over another

Equity: A stock or any other security representing an ownership interest

Factoring: A financing process in which a business sells some or all of its accounts receivable to a factoring company, thus giving the factoring company the right to collect the payment. The business sells the receivable at a discount to its value in exchange for immediate payment to the business

Fixed/Term Loan: A loan from a bank for a specific amount that has a specified repayment schedule

Free Cash Flow: The cash generated by a business that is available to repay debt and other obligations

Go-to-Market Strategy: The plan a company uses to effectively launch its product or service

Guarantee: A binding agreement between a borrower and a lender in which the borrower pledges to repay the loan amount in full.

- **Personal Guarantee**: A pledge made by the owner of a business that guarantees repayment of a loan. It is used to collateralize the loan and often includes a pledge of the personal assets of the individual making the guarantee for repayment in the event the business fails to repay its debt obligations
- **Business Guarantee**: A pledge made by the business itself (the legal entity) that guarantees repayment of a loan, it typically includes company assets used to collateralize the loan
- **Commercial Guarantee**: A legal document executed by the company that guarantees to the bank that they will be repaid. It generally included both a *business guarantee* and a *personal guarantee*

Hard Money Loans: A specific type of asset-based loan financing in which a borrower receives funds secured by real property

Income Statement: A financial statement that measures a company's financial performance (sales, cost of sales, expenses, and any profit loss) during a specific measurement period

Leverage: Using borrowed money to finance the growth of a company

Liquid Assets: Assets that can be converted to cash quickly; generally includes cash, marketable securities, and collectible accounts receivable

Liquidity: A measure of a company's liquid, or readily available, assets

Loan Loss Rate: The percentage of loans that do not get repaid to the bank

Measurement Period: The point in time or period of time over which a company's performance is measured

Military Reservist Economic Injury Disaster Loan Program: Specifically intended for veterans in the military reserves, this program provides extremely low interest loans to help you run the business if you are ever called to an extended period of active duty.

OPM: Short for 'other people's money,' allows you to share some of the risk with investors who contribute capital in the form of cash used to purchase equity in the company

Opportunity Cost: The lost opportunity, benefit, value, or income that could have been gained by selecting a different option. As it relates to bank loans, it is the income that could have been made by investing funds elsewhere

Peer to Peer (P2P) Lending: The practice of lending money to unrelated individuals, or "peers", without going through a traditional financial intermediary such as a bank or other traditional financial institution

Prohibited Business: Businesses that are restricted from receiving SBA financing, such as those that lend money, participate in multi-level marketing, or involve gambling or illegal activity

Promissory Note: A written agreement between parties in which one party promises to repay funds to the other

Qualitative Traits: Subjective or abstract aspects of a business that are difficult to measure and quantify, such as control and leadership

Quantitative Traits: Measurable /objective information such as growth rates and financial ratios

Real Property: Actual land and any structure built upon it

Revolving Line of Credit: Also known as a revolver, it is a line of credit set at an agreed upon limit which the business can draw from when funds are needed, up to the pre-approved limit

SBA Express Loan Program: A streamlined loan program that comes with a highly competitive rate and fairly quick turnaround time

Seed Funding: The first external funding a startup business raises, it is generally provided by friends and family or angel investors

Small Business Administration (SBA): A United States government agency that offers financing, loans, and other assistance to small businesses

Small Business Investment Companies (SBICs): Privately owned and managed organizations that use their own capital to invest in equity or make loans to small businesses

Source of Repayment: Funds the bank expects (under normal circumstances) will be used to repay the loan, most often in the form of the cash-flow generated by the business

Sources of Capital: Refers to the various financing options available to most businesses, each of which has distinct advantages and disadvantages

Subordinated Debt (Mezzanine Funding): Debt taken on by a company that is subordinated in repayment priority to senior debt owed to a bank or other lending institution

Underwriting: The process by which banks analyze, evaluate and document a loan prior to lending the funds. The underwriting process involves many steps to gauge the creditworthiness of the borrower, the likelihood of default and the establishment of multiple sources of collateral to ensure repayment of loaned funds.

Unsecured Loans: Loans that do not require specific collateral to support the loan; tend to be very costly because money is borrowed purely on your personal creditworthiness

Approved Study Guide Answer Key

Ch. 1

Answer Key

Vocabulary Match	*True or False*	*Fill in the Blank*
1. C	1. F	1. Local Community Banks; Regional/Multi-Regional Banks
2. E	2. F	2. Ancillary Services
3. A	3. F	3. Ancillary Services
4. B	4. F	4. Accommodating; Flexible
5. D	5. T	5. 50%; 20%
	6. T	6. Member-Owned
		7. Consumer Loans

Ch. 2

Answer Key

Vocabulary Match	*True or False*	*Fill in the Blank*
1. C	1. T	1. Relationship Banker
2. A	2. F	2. Credit Committee
3. B	3. F	3. Credit
4. E	4. F	4. Credit Officer
5. D	5. T	

Ch. 3

Answer Key

Vocabulary Match

1. J
2. C
3. E
4. I
5. K
6. A
7. F
8. B
9. D
10. H
11. G

True or False

1. T
2. F
3. T
4. F
5. F
6. F
7. T

Fill in the Blank

1. 10%;
   5%
2. Cheapest;
   Capital
3. Credit Cards
4. P2P Lending
5. Tax Benefit
6. Equity
7. Ownership
8. SBA
9. Flexibility
10. Increasing
11. Pro-Forma Projections;
    Business Plan
12. Bankable;
    Sources of Repayment
13. Collateral
14. SBICs

Ch. 4

Answer Key

Vocabulary Match	*True or False*	*Fill in the Blank*
1. E	1. T	1. Flexibility
2. D	2. F	2. Backs or Guarantees
3. A	3. F	3. Repayment Timeframe
4. B	4. T	4. Collateral
5. C	5. F	5. Businesses
	6. T	6. Taxes
	7. T	7. Express Loan Program
	8. F	8. Military Reservist Economic Injury Disaster Loan Program
	9. F	9. SBICs; Equity
	10. T	10. Impact Investments

Unit Review Test #1: Ch. 1 – 4

Answer Key

Vocabulary Match

1. F
2. K
3. H
4. E
5. A
6. I
7. C
8. B
9. J
10. D
11. G

True or False

1. F
2. F
3. F
4. F
5. T
6. T
7. F
8. F
9. T
10. T
11. F
12. F
13. T
14. T
15. T
16. T
17. F
18. T

Fill in the Blank/Multiple Choice

1. A
2. C
3. B
4. A
5. D
6. C
7. B
8. D
9. A
10. B
11. D
12. C
13. B
14. A
15. B
16. D
17. A
18. A
19. C
20. B

Ch. 5

Answer Key

Vocabulary Match	*True or False*	*Fill in the Blank*
1. F	1. T	1. Underwriting Process
2. J	2. T	2. Understand; Be Understood
3. H	3. F	3. Loan Loss Rate; 2%
4. A	4. F	4. Capacity; Capital; Conditions; Collateral; Character
5. D	5. T	5. Background
6. C	6. T	6. Executive Team; Company; Industry
7. L	7. F	7. Key Risks
8. E	8. F	8. Sources of Repayment; Collateral
9. I	9. T	9. Asset-Backed
10. B		10. Assignment of Claims
11. G		11. Primary Source of Repayment; Secondary Source of Repayment
12. K		12. Personal Guarantee
		13. Income Statement; Balance Sheet; Cash-Flow Statement

Ch. 6

Answer Key

Vocabulary Match

1. C
2. A
3. B

True or False

1. T
2. F
3. T
4. T

Fill in the Blank

1. Small Business Administration (SBA)
2. Term Loans;
   Revolving Lines of Credit
3. Revolving Line of Credit
4. Amortization Periods
5. Term Loan;
   Fixed

Ch. 7

Answer Key

Vocabulary Match

1. F
2. J
3. E
4. C
5. G
6. H
7. A
8. I
9. K
10. D
11. B

True or False

1. T
2. T
3. F
4. F
5. T
6. T
7. F

Fill in the Blank

1. Balance Sheet;
   Cash-Flow Statements
2. Historical Financial Statements
3. Pro-Forma
4. "Free" Cash-Flow;
   Working Capital Growth
5. Liabilities
6. 2-3 Years

Unit Review Test #2: Ch. 5 – 7

Answer Key

Vocabulary Match	*True or False*	*Fill in the Blank / Multiple Choice*
1. H	1. T	
2. G	2. T	1. B
3. M	3. F	2. D
4. I	4. F	3. A
5. D	5. F	4. B
6. B	6. T	5. C
7. F	7. F	6. A
8. A	8. F	7. D
9. K	9. T	8. C
10. E	10. T	9. A
11. C	11. F	10. B
12. L	12. T	11. D
13. J	13. T	12. A
14. N	14. T	13. B
	15. T	14. D
	16. F	15. C
	17. F	16. B
	18. T	17. A
	19. T	18. B
	20. F	

Ch. 8

Answer Key

Vocabulary Match	*True or False*	*Fill in the Blank*
1. G	1. F	1. Business Strategy
2. J	2. F	2. Roadmap to Success
3. C	3. F	3. Go-to-Market Strategy
4. E	4. T	4. Target Customers; Marketing Plan; Revenue Streams
5. A	5. F	5. Executive Summary
6. H	6. T	6. Summaries; Detailed Analyses
7. D	7. F	7. Industry; Market
8. I	8. T	8. Organization & Management Team Section
9. B	9. T	9. Market Penetration; Growth; Channels-of-Distribution; Communication
10. K	10. T	10. Appendices
11. F		

Ch. 9

Answer Key

Vocabulary Match

1. B
2. C
3. A
4. H
5. G
6. E
7. D
8. F

Covenant Calculations Exercise

Liquidity (Working Capital) Covenants

Name	Measures	Calculations	Covenant Requirement	Jessica's Value	In Compliance?
Current Ratio	Businesses short-term liquidity	CA / CL	Must remain greater that 1.5	1.23	NO
Quick Ratio	Businesses short-term liquidity	(CA - Inventory) / CL	Must remain greater than 1.0	1.07	YES

Profitability Covenants

Name	Measures	Calculations	Covenant Requirement	Jessica's Value	In Compliance?
Annual Net Income	Income produced during a particular measurement period	Value taken directly from Income Statement	Annual net income must be greater than $250,000	$255,357	YES
Quarterly Net Income	Income produced during a particular measurement period	Value taken directly from Income Statement	Quarterly net income must be greater than $0 - (No loss quarters)	-$8,699	NO

Leverage / Debt Coverage Covenants

Name	Measures	Calculations	Covenant Requirement	Jessica's Value	In Compliance?
Fixed Charge Coverage Ratio (FCC)	Ability to service debt with income generated by business	(NI+Int Exp+Lease Exp+Dep + Amort)/(Int Exp +Lease Exp + CPLTD)	Must remain greater than 1.20	1.17	NO

Notes:

Be sure not to double count capital lease expense in denominator of FCC calculation. [HINT: Look at CPLTD definition below.]

All values are calculated as of 6/30/16 using Jessica's Custom Clothing financial statements included above.

Code	Definitions	Covenant Code Key	Jessica's Value (at 6/30/19)
CA	Current Assets	A	$1,900,000
CL	Current Liabilities	B	$1,546,517
Inventory	Inventory	C	$250,000
NI (TTM)	Net Income	D (for last year (TTM))	$255,357
NI (Q2)	Net Income	E (for latest quarter - Q2)	-$8,699
EBITDA (TTM)	Earnings Before Interest, Taxes, Depreciation or Amortization	F (for last year (TTM))	$600,250
EBITDA (Q2)	Earnings Before Interest, Taxes, Depreciation or Amortization	O (for latest quarter - Q2)	$27,250
CPLTD	Current portion of LTD, including capital leases	G	$361,517
LTD	Long Term Debt, Including capital leases; Excluding Current Portion	H	$763,465
TD	Total Debt = All Debt Combined (CPLTD + LTD + LOC)	= G + H + P	$1,509,982
Lease Exp	Capital Lease Payments	I	$75,000
TA	Total Assets	J	$4,410,000
TL	Total Liabilities	K	$2,384,982
Net Worth	Net Worth = TA - TL	= J - K	$2,025,018
Int Exp	Interest Expense	L	$44,793
D&A	Depreciation & Amortization Expense	M	$100,000
Total Equity	Total Equity	N	$2,025,017
LOC	Line of Credit	P	$385,000

Ch. 10

Answer Key

Vocabulary Match	*True or False*	*Fill in the Blank*
1. B	1. T	1. Commercial / Corporate Guarantee
2. A	2. T	2. Spousal
3. D	3. T	3. Due Diligence
4. C	4. F	4. Commercial Guarantee; Personal Guarantee
	5. F	5. Personal Guarantee
	6. F	6. Unlimited
		7. Liabilities
		8. Bankable

Ch. 11

Answer Key

Fill in the Blank

1. Historical Financial Statements;
   Pro-Forma Projections
2. 3 to 5 years
3. Personal Financial Statement
4. Legal;
   Good Standing (CGS)
5. Repayment
   Collateral

Unit Review Test #3: Ch. 8 – 11

Answer Key

Vocabulary Match	*True or False*	*Fill in the Blank / Multiple Choice*
1. M	1. F	1. B
2. F	2. F	2. D
3. J	3. T	3. A
4. H	4. F	4. A
5. C	5. F	5. D
6. G	6. T	6. C
7. D	7. T	7. B
8. L	8. F	8. A
9. I	9. T	9. B
10. B	10. F	10. D
11. O	11. T	11. C
12. K	12. F	12. A
13. E	13. T	13. A
14. A	14. T	14. B
15. N	15. F	15. D
		16. C
		17. A
		18. B
		19. B
		20. C

Ch. 12

Answer Key

Vocabulary Match	*True or False*	*Fill in the Blank*
1. F	1. T	1. Small Business Lending Group (SBLG)
2. J	2. F	2. Corporate Resolution
3. I	3. T	3. Commercial Guarantee
4. B	4. F	4. Security Interest
5. G	5. T	5. Trust; Trustee; Beneficiaries
6. C		
7. E		
8. H		
9. A		
10. D		

Ch. 13

Answer Key

Vocabulary Match	*True or False*	*Fill in the Blank*
1. B	1. T	1. Contingencies
2. D	2. T	2. Business Strategy
3. C	3. T	3. Credit Rating Agencies
4. A	4. F	4. Communicate
	5. F	5. Relationships
	6. F	6. Credibility
	7. F	7. Likes; Trusts; Understand Your Business
	8. T	8. Highly Desirable; Every Bank
		9. Growth; Profitability
		10. Leverage

Ch. 14

Answer Key

Vocabulary	*True or False*	*Fill in the Blank*
1. C	1. F	1. Minor Violations
2. B	2. T	2. Fully analyze; Extent
3. A	3. T	3. Corrective Action Plan
	4. T	4. Incentive; Credit Risk
	5. F	5. Responsibility
		6. Forbearance Agreement; Short-term

Ch. 16

Answer Key

Vocabulary Match	*True or False*	*Fill in the Blank*
1. D	1. T	1. Bootstrapping
2. M	2. F	2. Opportunity Cost
3. A	3. T	3. Cash on Hand or Readily Available
4. G	4. F	4. Liquid Assets
5. B	5. T	5. Emergency Fund
6. H	6. F	6. Friends & Family
7. L	7. F	7. Personal (Unsecured); Third Parties
8. E	8. F	8. Peer-to-Peer (P2P) Lending; Portals
9. F		9. Credit Cards; Credit Limits
10. C		10. Subordinated (Mezzanine)
11. K		11. Credit Card Teaser Rates; Home Equity Lines of Credit (HELOCs)
12. I		12. Equity; Capital
13. N		13. Ownership; Control
14. J		14. Future Potential
		15. Lack of Collateral; Insufficient Sources of Repayment
		16. Crowdfunding

Unit Review Test #4: Ch. 12 – 16

Answer Key

Vocabulary Match

1. L
2. I
3. Q
4. C
5. J
6. K
7. N
8. D
9. M
10. O
11. S
12. F
13. U
14. A
15. G
16. B
17. H
18. V
19. R
20. T
21. W
22. X
23. E
24. P

True or False

1. T
2. T
3. F
4. T
5. T
6. T
7. F
8. F
9. F
10. T
11. F
12. T
13. T
14. F
15. T
16. T
17. F
18. T
19. F
20. F

Fill in the Blank / Multiple Choice

1. B
2. A
3. D
4. C
5. B
6. A
7. B
8. D
9. C
10. A
11. C
12. B
13. A
14. A
15. B
16. A
17. C
18. B

About Alan Stewart

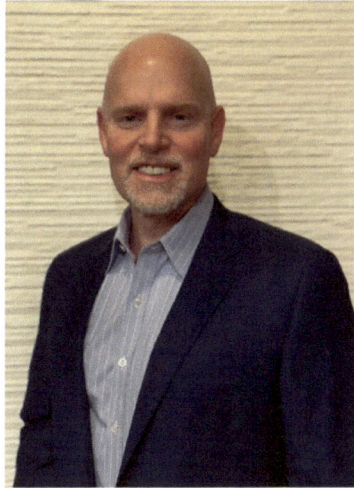

Since 2017 Alan R. Stewart has served as Chief Financial Officer of ShotSpotter, Inc., a Silicon Valley-based public SaaS software company that he took public on the NASDAQ in 2017. From May 2015 to February 2017, Mr. Stewart was a Managing Director of RA Capital Advisors, LLC, a private investment bank specializing in mergers and acquisitions, private financings and restructurings. He has also served in business development for a commercial bank focused on loans to middle market commercial clients.

From 2004 to 2014, he served as Chief Financial Officer and then Chief Development Officer of Epsilon Systems Solutions, Inc. Since 2008, Mr. Stewart has served as President & CEO of FIT Advisors, LLC, a boutique consulting firm that has offered temporary CFO and board services and served clients from start-up ventures to large private companies.

Mr. Stewart was selected as San Diego Business Journal's CFO of the Year in 2007 and again in 2013. Both awards were in the large private business category. Mr. Stewart was selected as BNY Mellon's 2017 Advisor of the Year in San Diego in the category of "Deal Facilitator Greater than $25M." Mr. Stewart was also nominated as CFO of the Year for San Francisco Bay area & Silicon Valley public companies in 2018 and 2019.

Prior to his business career, Mr. Stewart served over ten years as a submarine nuclear engineer in the United States Navy. He received his B.S. in Oceanography, with distinction, from the U.S. Naval Academy and his M.B.A. from Harvard Business School.

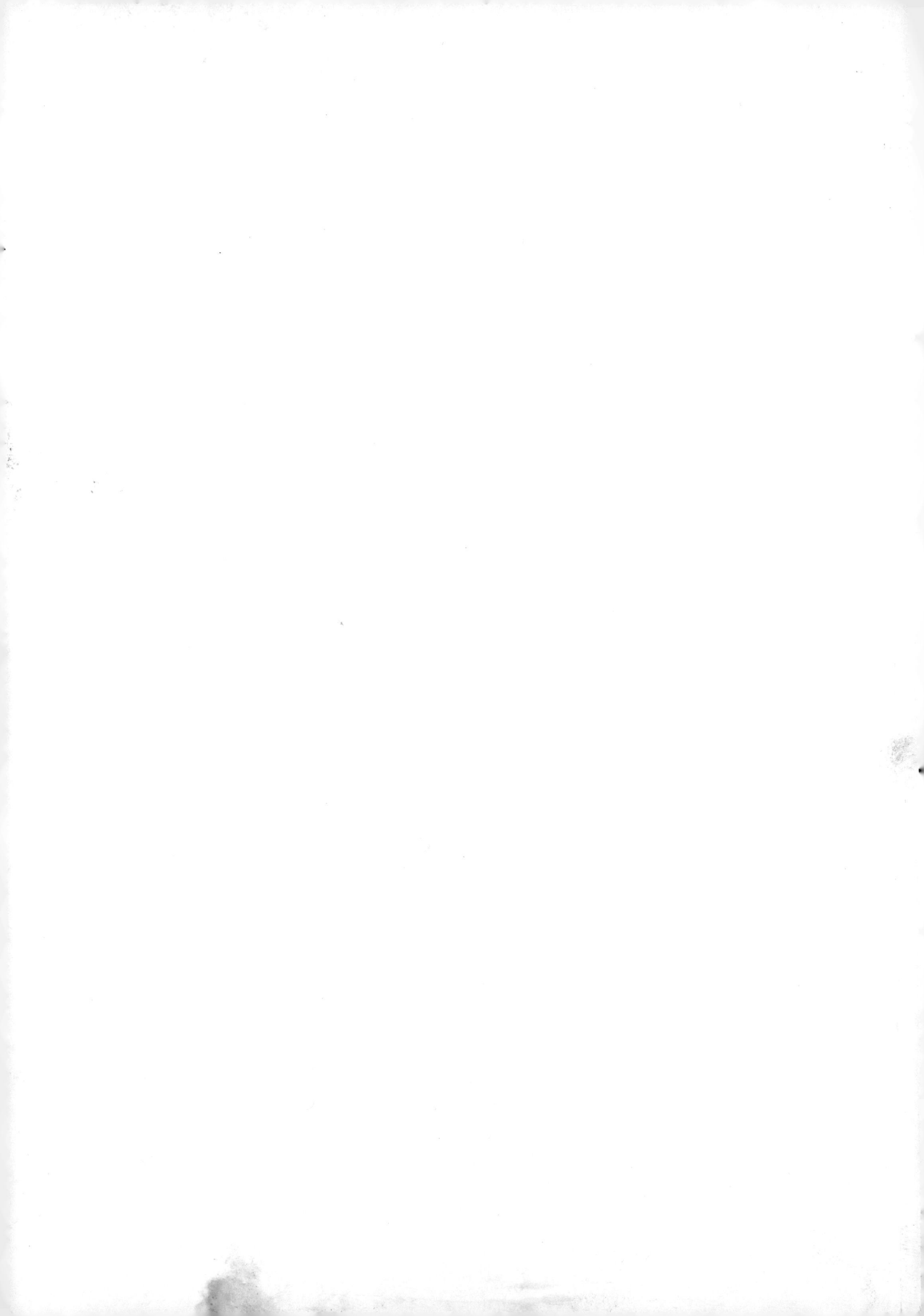